RIPPER
SUSPECT

RIPPER SUSPECT

THE SECRET LIVES OF MONTAGUE DRUITT

D. J. LEIGHTON

SUTTON PUBLISHING

First published in the United Kingdom in 2006 by
Sutton Publishing Limited · Phoenix Mill
Thrupp · Stroud · Gloucestershire · GL5 2BU

British Library Cataloguing in Publication Data
A catalogue record for this book is available from the British Library.

ISBN 0-7509-4329-7

Typeset in 11/14.5pt Sabon.
Typesetting and origination by
Sutton Publishing Limited.
Printed and bound in England by
J.H. Haynes & Co. Ltd, Sparkford.

To Ann, with love

Contents

Acknowledgements

So many people have helped me put together this book that it is beyond me to thank them all. However the following have indeed given me great assistance.

My thanks to

Nick Baker, Simon Berry, Marijke Booth, Peter Brown, John Carter, Peter Cattrall, Tony Connor, Susan Cornelius, Angela Crean, Ernest Crump, Ken Daldry, Caroline Dalton, Carol Ann Dickson, Steve Dingvean, David Dongworth, David Fellowes, Dave Froggatt, Robert Fyson, Brian Gibbons, Nick Gibbs, Stephen Green, Jeffrey Hancock, Stawell Heard, Bob Holmes, Neil Holmes, Clare Hopkins, Morley Howell, Jim Hunter, Trevor Jones, Margaret Knight, Bryan Lloyd, Giles Lyon, David and Pamela McCleave, James McDermott, Patrick Maclure, Prakesh Makwana, Warren Martin, Peter Nicholls, Carl Openshaw, Tim Prager, Elaine Quigley, Neil Rhind, Irving Rosenwater, Lindsay Siviter, Jeff Smith, Robert Smith, Mark Stanford, Bert Street, Sara Tutton, May Valentine, John Whittall, Richard Wileman, Murray and Myra Wrobel.

I am also indebted to individuals and organisations who allowed me to use their photographs. To anyone to whom acknowledgements are due, but who has been unintentionally overlooked, I offer my apologies and an assurance that this will be put right in later editions.

D.J. Leighton

List of Illustrations

ONE

The Scene is Set

In the autumn of 1888 in the Whitechapel area of east London five appalling murders took place. All the victims were prostitutes; four of them were mutilated and parts of their bodies removed. The nature of the crimes led the police to believe that they were the work of one person. Then taunting letters began to arrive, signed by someone calling himself 'Jack the Ripper'. This was a nasty but accurate description of the murderer's work. The killings became known as the Jack the Ripper murders, and the obloquy has helped to ensure that the case has remained high in the general public's awareness to this day.

Since the mid-1990s, forty new books on the subject have been published. This is higher than for any other true-life crime. Patricia Cornwell's *Portrait of a Killer* demonstrates the huge interest that continues to exist in the subject. The paperback edition was an international bestseller, topped the *Sunday Times* lists for six weeks and sold over 150,000 copies between September 2003 and the end of that year. Even today the Ripper's frightening spectre retains its power. In May 2005 Michael Winner, writing his restaurant column

1

also in the *Sunday Times*, recorded that his friend Paola Lombard disliked the small Italian village of Apricale. She thought the narrow, cobbled streets 'were spooky'. 'I expect to meet Jack the Ripper any moment,' she said. Some writers and historians have listed as many as twelve victims of the Ripper, but five is the generally accepted number.

This, briefly, is a summary of those murders.

The first woman to die was Mary Ann Nichols, who was found on Friday, 31 August, at about 3.30 a.m. near a Kearley and Tonge warehouse in Bucks Row (now Durward Street), her body slashed and mutilated. Nichols had been born in 1845 in east London and by the time she was 19 she was married to William Nichols, a printer. This relationship produced five children but ended in 1880, partly because of her heavy drinking. For the rest of her life she lived mostly in workhouses, slept rough or rented the cheapest room in the worst areas of the East End. Earlier that Friday night she had boasted to a friend about her successful earnings that evening. She was drunk. Her body was identified a few hours later by her husband and the same family friend, Emily Holland. The police surgeon who carried out the post-mortem was Dr Ralph Llewellyn and the coroner was Wynne Baxter. At first Llewellyn believed the murderer was left-handed but later he became less sure. He was, however, firm in his opinion that the killer 'must have some anatomical knowledge'. He commented, 'I have never seen so horrible a case.'

The second victim was 47-year-old Annie Chapman, who died at about 5.30 a.m. on Saturday, 8 September, in Hanbury Street, which leads into Commercial Street. At one time she had been married, with three children, to a coachman, John Chapman, in Windsor, but they had separated in 1884 and she had moved to Whitechapel, where she sold flowers, did some sewing and worked the streets at nights. Between times she drank in local pubs. On the night of her murder she had been plying her trade to make money for her room. This time the police surgeon handling the post-mortem was Dr George Bagster Phillips. It was his view that there had been an attempt at decapitation, but in any event her body had been horribly cut up, and it was clear to Dr Phillips that the assailant had medical knowledge of anatomy and pathology. The coroner as for the first victim was Wynne Baxter and he agreed with these findings. He also drew attention to the removal of body parts.

On Sunday, 30 September, two Ripper murders took place and these became known as the 'Double Event'. The first to die was Elizabeth Stride, who was killed at about 1.00 a.m. in Dutfield's Yard, near the Commercial Road. Stride was born in Sweden in 1843, and became involved in prostitution at the age of 21. In 1866 she moved to London, married a John Stride three years later, and went to live in Clerkenwell. In 1878 the pleasure steamer *Princess Alice* sank in the River Thames and 527 lives were lost. Stride invented the story that her husband and children were among the victims, but in fact John Stride died in the Poplar Union Workhouse in 1884, three years after the marriage had ended. Elizabeth Stride now reverted to her old profession, and in the hours before her death had spent the time drinking and soliciting. Again Dr Phillips held the post-mortem and Wynne Baxter was the coroner. Death was by a cut to the throat, and Baxter believed the murderer 'knew where to cut'. The absence of mutilation suggested to the coroner that the killer had been disturbed, but the death is still attributed to the Ripper.

On the same night about half an hour after the murder of Elizabeth Stride another woman was killed a few hundred yards away in Mitre Square. The Kearley and Tonge head office occupied two sides of the Square, so it was the second time a victim had been found near Kearley and Tonge premises. Her name was Catherine Eddowes, aged 46, and she had been brought up as an orphan in a workhouse. She settled in Whitechapel with a soldier Thomas Conway with whom she had three children, but the relationship ended in 1880 partly because of Eddowes's alcoholism. She soon moved in with John Kelly, a labourer, and became variously known as Eddowes, Conway and Kelly. Although extremely poor, she may have been a casual, rather than a career, prostitute, and the two scraped a living doing agricultural work. The time prior to the murder is well documented as she had been in police custody until 1.00 a.m. sobering up from a drinking binge. Within an hour of her release she was dead; her throat had been cut, her body slashed and parts removed. Dr Frederick Gordon Brown carried out the post-mortem and noted: 'I believe the perpetrator of the act must have had considerable knowledge of the position of the organs. It would have needed great knowledge.' Eddowes's death had all the hallmarks of an authentic Ripper murder. There is, however, a possibility that the murder was a mistake, as she may not have been a regular prostitute and could have been confused with the fifth victim.

The last of the five women to be killed was Mary Jane Kelly in the early hours of Friday, 9 November, in Miller's Court, near Commercial Street. Her background and life were desperate. Born in Limerick in 1862, she moved to Wales and married a coal miner called Jonathan Davies when she was 16. Within months Davies was killed in a pit accident, and Kelly was introduced to prostitution in Cardiff by her aunt. In 1884 she moved to London and worked partly in a gentlemen's gay club and partly in a West End brothel. Eventually she moved to the East End, an even more degrading environment, where she continued to ply her trade. She was last seen at about 1.00 a.m. on the Friday morning the worse for drink. Her body was found cut up almost beyond identification, and of all the murders this was the most gruesome. Dr Phillips again did the post-mortem and Mr Roderick MacDonald was the coroner.

These then are the five murders. The only motives can have been a gruesome sexual gratification, a twisted mission against prostitutes or an urge to silence certain people. All were too poor to be robbed. No one was ever charged or convicted, and, although dozens of men were interviewed, the investigation progressed no further.

There was no shortage of candidates, even claimants. The *Lewisham Gazette* of 7 December 1888 reported under the headline 'Jack the Ripper in a Fish Shop' that a John Weidon of Francis Street, Woolwich, had entered a fish shop owned by Mr and Mrs Seagain in New Cross Road. On being refused credit, Weidon began to smash up bottles and plates and threatened, 'I am Jack the Ripper and will do for you.' He was fined 10s (50p) with 2s costs, or seven days in prison.

Six years later the Chief Constable of the Metropolitan area, Sir Melville Macnaghten, named Montague Druitt as the murderer, but by then Druitt was dead. Nevertheless, for the last 100 years Druitt's name has been inextricably linked with that of Jack the Ripper. This book tells the life of Montague Druitt, and the circumstances that surrounded him. It examines the validity of Macnaghten's claim in the light of this evidence.

At the time of the murders, the East End of London had a population approaching a million, of which some 80,000 lived in the Whitechapel area. The East End as a whole was an area of abject poverty and dreadful living conditions. Charles Dickens had placed his characters Fagin and Bill Sikes in Whitechapel, the seediest part of London he knew. To see starving and dying people on the streets was not uncommon. The small squalid houses were hopelessly overcrowded, and often there was a room occupancy of six or more people. There was no large-scale industry such as mills or other manufacturing to sustain the people who would have gained such employment in the northern cities. There was some work for men in the London docks, but this was fiercely controlled so that only those perceived as being English could participate. The railways, too, provided limited work, but mostly men relied on occasional building jobs, street trading or hard manual labour, working long hours for £1 per week. Much of the population was drifting and rootless. Jewish and Eastern European enclaves were formed, and itinerant sailors up from the docks came and went. Nor did it help that gang warfare had arrived early in the nineteenth century, and by the 1880s groups of thugs such as the Old Nichol Gang, the Blind Beggar Mob, the Green Gate Gang and the Hoxton Mob were roaming the streets. Some gangs were formed along ethnic lines, and their presence added to the frightening reputation of the area.

The most common form of work for women was making or finishing cheap clothes in conditions that amounted to sweated labour. If she was lucky, a woman could earn 1s (5p) for 12 hours' work. This would typically involve sewing on buttons, edging trousers or making buttonholes. For many their working lives began when they were still children, and inevitably these conditions led to a drift to prostitution for a large section of the society. Even married women, or those in some sort of relationship, often resorted to part-time or opportunistic prostitution. At the time of the killings the Metropolitan Police believed there were 1,200 full-time prostitutes and fifty brothels in Whitechapel alone, and many more women were casual operators. A few years earlier the medical magazine the *Lancet* had put the number of London prostitutes of one sort or another at 80,000. It was a figure with which the Bishop of Exeter agreed. For large sections of poverty-stricken London women it was the main industry, despite the pathetically low charges that these women made. With all this activity came high rates of venereal disease, alcoholism and early death; alcohol featured significantly in the lives of all five of the victims and the best that social security could provide was workhouses and doss houses. As there was no local mortuary, the bodies of the murdered women were taken to a shed next to the workhouse for the post-mortems, where they rapidly decomposed. Jack London, the American crime writer, called the area 'the Abyss'. But if Whitechapel was the worst area of the East End in terms of squalor, poverty and the absence of adequate medical help, the worst street of all in Whitechapel was Flower and Dean Street. Four of the murders took place in its immediate vicinity. In 1885 it was described by James Greenwood, a social commentator, as 'what is perhaps the foulest and most dangerous street in the whole metropolis'. Later there were some attempts to demolish it, but it took German bombers finally to remove it in 1917.

Although these conditions produced widespread crime, it was mostly petty in nature and murders were unusual. The year before the Ripper killings, there was none in Whitechapel. However, in 1888 at least seven prostitutes were killed. Something peculiar was going on, and it led the police to the view that all or most of the crimes were the work of one madman. As a community Whitechapel did not appreciate its increased notoriety. Bands of men were formed into vigilante groups, and the women raised a petition of 4,000 signatures in three days, which they succeeded in bringing to the attention of Queen Victoria. Her reply was not especially helpful. A spokesman bore the message that 'the Queen is desirous that those interested should know how much she sympathised'. Up to now Victoria's record for espousing women's causes was non-existent. A few years earlier she had proclaimed: 'Feminists ought to get a good whipping. Were women to unsex themselves by claiming equality with men, they would become the most hateful, heathen and disgusting of beings and would surely perish without more protection.' After the fifth murder she did take matters more seriously and sent an instruction to Prime Minister Salisbury: 'This new ghastly murder shows the absolute necessity for some very decided action.' Earlier the Queen had acknowledged conditions in the East End. In 1883 she wrote to Prime Minister Gladstone asking him to 'obtain more precise information as to the true state of affairs in these overcrowded, unhealthy and squalid abodes'. Public meetings, sometimes with religious overtones, defended the people of east London, whose reputation anyway was most unattractive. One gathering ended by proclaiming that the meeting had 'no confidence in the present management of the police'. The docklands trade unions waded in with an offer to 'place seventy trained working men on the streets of Whitechapel from 10.00 p.m. until 7.00 a.m. Such men full of courage and endurance might well prove to be the means of capturing the villain.' The unions did expect some sort of financial reward for their members' efforts, however, and when this was slow in materialising the offer faded away.

Despite the efforts of such groups, sometimes not entirely altruistic, to put an end to the murders and restore a vestige of self-respect to the area, the East End was and remained an area of awful social conditions. It was characterised by nasty little gas-lit streets, grim, damp tenements and uniform deprivation. This created the environment in which hundreds of women put their lives at risk every night. As a contemporary writer put it, 'they sell themselves for thru'pence or tu'pence or a stale loaf of bread'. The October 1888 edition of the *British Medical Journal* thundered its condemnation of the East End's conditions: 'We have had the heavy fringes of a vast population packed into dark places, festering in ignorance, in dirt, in moral degradation, accustomed to violence and crime, born and bred within touch of habitual immorality and coarse obscenity.' It was a most legitimate summary.

TWO

Almost a Dynasty

On Saturday, 8 September 1888, Montague Druitt was a worried man. He was playing cricket against the Christopherson Brothers' team in the end-of-season inter-club match at the Rectory Field, Blackheath, and it was his turn to bat. Two wickets had gone cheaply and it was not yet midday. Opposing him was the former England opening bowler, Stanley Christopherson, who was fast and accurate, but batting had never been Montague's main strength, and at no. 4 in the batting order he did not feel equipped to deal with the threatening pace. He was right, and Christopherson soon sent him on his way back to the pavilion. Later on Montague redeemed himself by taking 3 wickets and finishing on the winning side. His last act on a cricket field was to bowl Derman Christopherson, the father of the side. Moments later Frederick Ireland bowled the youngest son, also called Derman, and the match was over. In the usual highly convivial end-of-season celebration everyone would have forgotten Montague's brief innings, and anyway he was a popular and respected member of one of the leading amateur sides in the land. Hopefully he enjoyed the moment, for unbeknown to him at the age of 31 his cricket career, the joy of his life, was over. He would never set foot on a cricket field again.

Meanwhile, 6 miles away in Whitechapel, Dr George Bagster Phillips, the Divisional Police surgeon, was having a much worse day. At 6.15 a.m. he had been woken by Inspector Joseph Chandler of the Metropolitan H Division summoning him to deal with the dismembered corpse of a woman. Dr Phillips, an experienced surgeon in his fifties, drew up a gruesomely anatomical account of what lay before him. His report on the dead woman Annie Chapman was presented at the inquest five days later. Dr Phillips stated that the removal of some body parts would have needed professional skills, and if he had been carrying out the surgery for an autopsy it would have taken him an hour. As if Dr Phillips's task was not unpleasant enough, he received a reprimand for not relating even more details of the wounds.

While Montague was taking some brisk and enjoyable exercise at the Rectory Field, Dr Phillips was writing his report. Such were its contents that after twenty-six blameless years as a police surgeon he was no longer enjoying his work. But over the next three months, life for Dr Phillips was to get much worse, and by the end of the year his unenviable, if small, place in criminal history would be ensured. It was to be his grim duty to attend the inquests for four of the five victims; his findings and opinions were central to the subsequent hunt for the murderer.

Montague John Druitt was born on 15 August 1857 at Westfield House in Wimborne, Dorset. Six weeks later he was christened at the Minster by the Revd William Mayo, a brother of Montague's grandmother. The Mayo family and its connections became of interest much later in the quest to unravel the legends and mysteries of Montague's life and death.

Montague was the third child of William and Ann Druitt. William was a doctor and surgeon with the largest practice in Wimborne, which he had mostly taken over from his father. Both were members of the Royal College of Surgeons. Ann had been brought up close by in Shapwick also in a professional family and was well off in her own right. At the time of their marriage in June 1854 she was 27 and William ten years older. They soon set about raising a family and produced seven children in the next seventeen years. Their first child was a girl, Georgiana, followed a year later by William Harvey (Ann's maiden name) and then Montague. Four more children soon followed – Edward, Arthur, Edith and lastly, in 1871, Ethel.

Westfield House was a fine, solid early Victorian manor set in a magnificent six-acre estate, which included stables, where the horses and carriages were kept, and two cottages for the servants. Today it still stands between Westfield Close and Redcotts Lane, divided into eight flats. Apart from the property of Lord and Lady Wimborne, it was the best house in the town.

Nearby, Wimborne Minster still bears an impressive five-lighted window presented to the church by the family of William and Ann Druitt. It is in the south transept and, appropriate to a doctor, has as its theme the treatment of the sick. St Luke, Isaiah, St Christopher, St John and Ezekiel are all depicted in various acts of healing. It was dedicated in the early 1890s and was probably the work of either John Clayton or Nathaniel Lavers, two of the best stained-glass glaziers of the time. Some years earlier a smaller window had been dedicated to William Druitt's father, Robert. This window shows St Luke and St Cuthburga, the foundress of Wimborne Minster. Abbess Cuthburga, the sister of King Ine of Wessex, separated in mid-life from her husband, Aldfrith, King of Northumbria, to set up the community at Wimborne. Cuthburga is still the ecclesiastical name for the parish. The windows serve as a reminder of the status of the Druitts in the town and of their commitment to the church and the medical profession.

Montague was brought up in style and comfort in a gentle pastoral setting, quite unaware that not all Victorian England, especially the East End of London, was similarly privileged. William Druitt was a disciplinarian with traditional Victorian views. He was a governor of the ancient Queen Elizabeth Grammar School, which had been founded by Lady Margaret, the mother of Henry VII, in the late fifteenth century. He was a trustee or treasurer of many local charities at the Board of Guardians, was Chairman of the Governing

Body of the Minster and was, according to the *Wimborne Guardian*, 'a strong churchman and a conservative'. He was also a Justice of the Peace. The only story to cloud his reputation was a rumour that, when his sons had left home, he used the spare rooms as a private mental hospital for patients from the aristocracy. In keeping with the times, the four sons were duly sent to leading public schools, and an Oxford education would be expected to follow. Montague went to Winchester, Edward to Cheltenham, Arthur to Marlborough and William to Clifton. At Clifton William was a pupil of John Percival, Clifton's founding headmaster. The girls' education is not recorded, but, again in keeping with the times, they were probably sent to local day schools or given a governess.

Up the road at Christchurch, William Druitt's brother Robert, also a doctor, was bringing up his own family of ten children, including a son, Lionel, who would be suspected of playing a part in the intrigue that surrounded Montague after his death. Another cousin of Montague, Herbert Druitt, became fascinated by local history and built up a huge collection of artefacts. His obsessive collection included fossils, stuffed birds, books, papers, china, paintings, drawings, photographs, fashion plates, brass rubbings and textiles. His ambition was to open a museum. Herbert died in 1943, but eight years later, when all the material had been sorted, the Red House Museum was opened and remains so to this day. It stands near Christchurch Priory on the site of the old parish workhouse. Prized among its paintings is a small oil by Henry Scott Tuke, entitled *The Cabin Boy*. It has always puzzled the museum's curator Jim Hunter how a picture of such quality came into Herbert's possession. The Christchurch public library also bears the Druitt name in large letters over its doorway.

At home at Westfield House, the main influences on Montague's life would have been his father, mother and his elder brother William. He would also have had an interest in Edward as he grew up, mainly because of his cricketing skills, which probably exceeded his own. Edward played a full season in the Cheltenham side at the age of 16 and was the leading wicket-taker. Charles Alcock, the editor of *James Lillywhite's Cricketers' Annual*, described him as 'a straight medium paced bowler. A fair bat; lacks energy' – a strange comment on a man who was to spend his next thirty years in the British Army. The next year Alcock was kinder and described his batting as 'greatly improved' and recorded that he had the 'best bowling analysis of the year'. At Cheltenham he was highly regarded. The school magazine, *The Cheltonian*, noted in its issue dated March 1876 that 'Hayes and Druitt are going up for examination next term, so will not be available to play in all cricket matches, which will weaken the eleven'.

Like Montague at Winchester, Edward occasionally confronted a player who would prove exceptional. In 1875 in a match against Marlborough Edward bowled against A.G. Steel, who as England captain retained the Ashes. Steel also took two centuries off the Australians and served as President of MCC.

Edward was the only one of the brothers who did not go to university. From Cheltenham he went to the Royal Military Academy, Woolwich, and then into the Royal Engineers. Both establishments afforded great opportunities to play good cricket. Edward served with the Royal Engineers until his retirement from the army in 1909; he had reached the rank of Lieutenant-Colonel. Afterwards he worked for several years for the Board of Trade investigating railway accidents. This must have seemed mundane after the camaraderie of an army life. However, he and his wife Christina had to endure one personal tragedy: on 9 May 1915 their only son, Edward, was killed at Ypres. He was a 2nd Lieutenant with the 2nd Royal Berkshire Regiment, and like his father he had made the army his life. His death was recorded in *The Times*, 17 May 1915, under the headline 'Fallen Officers'. The same report carried details of the death, also at Ypres, of Major the Honourable Clement Mitford, of the 10th Hussars, traditionally the regiment of aristocrats and royalty. He was the uncle of Diana Mitford, later to be Lady Oswald Mosley.

Montague's elder brother, William, was also a useful cricketer. Like Montague he played for Bournemouth and Kingston Park, and in a match at Bournemouth in 1877 he dismissed Montague. When he went up to Oxford, he was good enough to play in the

Freshmen's Match, a trial match for those in their first year at Oxford. William took 4 wickets, but it was insufficient and he played no further visible part in university cricket. Montague had already left home to become a boarder at Winchester when Ethel, his youngest sister, was born early in 1871. Movement and change characterised life at Westfield House as the seven children came and went between school, university and their careers. For Montague the new challenge of Winchester and beyond had begun.

THREE

'Manners Makyth Man'

When Montague set off to Winchester College in January 1870, he did so as a fee-paying pupil and entered Fearon's, the house named after William Fearon, a housemaster who later became headmaster. After two terms Montague achieved a scholarship, coming third among all scholars, and this relieved his father of paying his fees. He had been identified as one of the brightest boys, and bypassed the junior part of the school to enter College in the middle section. He progressed very well, and attained the distinction of being taught by the headmaster, Dr George Ridding, for the last three years. Academically he was a star. It was the same Dr Ridding who had given cricket at Winchester an enormous boost when, in 1869, he presented the school with a piece of ground called Lavender Meads. It became the new cricket ground, to be known as Ridding Field, and Montague was one of the lucky beneficiaries.

Montague was also extremely good at games. By the time he was 16 he was playing regularly in the school's cricket 2nd XI. Although a rather wild fast bowler at the time, he did well in the prestigious internal matches such as the Two Guinea Match and the

15

match against The Next Sixteen. In 1876 he was in the 1st XI and most notably played against Eton, a side that contained the Hon. Ivo Bligh (later the 8th Lord Darnley). Bligh captained England on the tour to Australia in 1882–3 and recovered the Ashes lost so ignominiously at the Oval in 1882. Also in the Eton side was J.E.K. (Kynaston) Studd, who was already a very good player. He went on to win four Blues at Cambridge, played for Middlesex and the MCC, and in 1928 became Lord Mayor of London. Montague bowled him for 4. Included in the same Eton side was Evelyn Ruggles-Brise, who was to crop up at regular intervals in Montague's life, and who later, as Private Secretary to the Home Secretary, knew the secrets and theories about the Ripper murders. As such he had an influence on Montague's posthumous reputation. On a happier note, *Wisden* records that, at the match played at Winchester, 'The Hospitality of the Head Master of England's oldest public school was as great, if not greater, than on former occasions.' A fortnight earlier on 8 June, the MCC had played at Winchester, and among their players was the legendary Alfred Shaw – one of the pivotal players of nineteenth-century cricket. Less than a year later he bowled the first ball in Test cricket at Melbourne. He traversed the pre- and post-Test Match eras with huge acumen. Although the report does not say if Montague faced Shaw, *Wisden* does give Montague a small note of distinction: 'Mr Druitt's seventeen, included 3 3's and his nine not out, a 5 and a 3.' Merely to have been on the same field as Shaw would have been a great thrill and honour for a young man like Montague. Montague was beginning to move among people who would make a mark in the upper echelons of society. Unwittingly he was building up a list of social contacts.

It is not true that Montague ever played at Lord's, the headquarters of cricket. The misunderstanding occurs because boys who played in the 1st XI were known as Lords. Furthermore, the venue for the Butterflies Cricket Club fixture against the Old Wykehamists is given in the 2003 fixture list as Lords, Winchester. Had Montague attended Winchester a generation earlier, he would indeed have played at Lord's. For many years up to 1854 the

Eton–Winchester match was always played there, and it was a great day out for the boys. Unfortunately the day became rather too much fun, and, following some riotous behaviour at Waterloo Station in 1854, the Headmaster banned the match. The fixture of course continues, but on a more mundane home-and-away basis. It is a fixture with a great tradition. The first Eton–Winchester match was played on Hounslow Heath in 1796, and it was some forty years later that it switched to Lord's. The first time Winchester ever played at Lord's the aftermath was the most disastrous episode in the history of Lord's ground. In the early hours of 29 July 1825, following a match between Winchester and Harrow, the pavilion caught fire and was completely destroyed. Precious possessions, records, trophies and scorebooks were lost. Even the wine cellar, which kept private supplies for members, did not escape, and the whole structure was reduced to a heap of ruins in 90 minutes. Undaunted, the Eton–Harrow match was played as scheduled less than 12 hours later. On this occasion no suggestion of blame was attached to the Winchester pupils. Arson, although never proved, was suspected, since there were no open fires in the pavilion in the summer, only a candle for cigar lighting. A new pavilion was built the following year.

A colleague at Winchester whom Montague got to know well was Herbert Webbe. He was the brother of the Harrovian Alexander Webbe, and both had excellent cricketing careers. On leaving school the three of them came together at Oxford. It was at Winchester, however, through Herbert, that one of the school's enduring legends was born. At the age of 30 Herbert collapsed and died of a heart attack while conducting prayers. Although he had shown symptoms of heart problems during his last year at Oxford, these were thought to have cleared, and he was leading a normal energetic life. His death was therefore most unexpected and a terrible blow to the Webbe family. It also affected Montague, as he had known Herbert for many years, and they had often played together in the same cricket side. Webbe's parents decided that they would present Winchester College with a cricket pavilion dedicated to their son's memory. In the language of Winchester this became known as

Webbe Tent, since up to then marquees had always served as pavilions. The Tent survived for many years, but eventually in 1930 a new larger one was needed with extra facilities. This time an offer to fund the new pavilion came from the Hunter family, whose male members had been educated at Winchester for two generations. It was to commemorate three members of the family – Robert, Richard and Hugh – who had died at a very young age. (Richard and Hugh perished in France in the First World War.) The Hunter family did realise the sensitivity of the Webbe name and the history behind the naming of the pavilion, so they requested it should continue to be known as Webbe Tent. The day of the opening ceremony arrived, and Alexander Webbe, now aged 75, agreed to open the new pavilion. Webbe was conscious of the situation and without recourse to anyone announced in his speech: 'I declare the pavilion open, and it shall be known as Hunter Tent.' It was the very essence of the school's motto 'Manners Makyth Man'. The pavilion and its name still survive.

Montague occasionally made useful runs but he was certainly a better bowler. The *Lillywhite's Annual* recording the season of 1876 bluntly assessed his performance in the Winchester XI: 'M.J. Druitt as a bat did not excel, his style was quite peculiar to himself. Bowled very much better than ever before and was a very useful man in the XI.' Lillywhite might have added that he was a fine outfielder with a huge throw, which had won him third place in the Throwing the Cricket Ball sports day event. Physically he was big and strong and good at most ball games. He played football, won the Wigram's Cup for rackets doubles and the singles and doubles Fives competitions. There is still a silver cup in the College Plate collection that Montague won in an Under-16 Fives tournament in 1873. The ambidexterity needed for Fives was, some years later, used to implicate Montague in the Whitechapel murders.

If Druitt had a weakness at school, it was acting. He put in one appearance for the Shakespeare Society as Sir Toby Belch in *Twelfth Night*. The theatre critic of *The Wykehamist* magazine was not impressed. He wrote: 'but of the inadequacy of Druitt as Sir Toby what are we to say? It can better be imagined than described.'

The day-to-day regime at Winchester was harsh. Ronald Pearsall in his book *The Worm in the Bud* describes how the newest arrival at Winchester, known as 'junior in chambers', had to light fires without the use of tongs. To 'toughen' him in this task he was given 'tin gloves'. This was a ritual involving an older boy taking a red hot iron and branding the young boy's fingers and wrists. If the boy still could not light the fire, the process was repeated.

Lord Alfred Douglas, who went to the College slightly after Montague in 1884, described his early time there: 'I came in for the last year of real savagery . . . it was a sink of inquity . . . my first eighteen months there were pretty much of a nightmare.' When Douglas left Winchester, he was uncompromising in his self-assessment: 'I left Winchester neither better nor worse than my contemporaries – that is to say a finished young blackguard, ripe for any kind of wickedness. My moral sense was completely destroyed and as to religion it was treated with contempt, ridicule and blasphemy.' His saving grace seems to have been an ability to run well, and in view of his later predicament this may have been a useful asset in more ways than one.

Masters and senior boys often administered floggings as public ceremonies. Winchester had its own special cane made of four apple twigs tied to a wooden handle. The weapon was then impregnated with grease and heated to toughen it, so that, in the words of a naturalist, 'it was as tough as a whalebone.' A contemporary said of Dr Ridding, 'It was not unusual of him after morning school to castigate not less than fifty boys at a time.' During three years of close proximity to Dr Ridding it would be surprising if Montague did not experience the apple twigs a few times. Among the leading public schools flogging approached an art form, and masters from different schools met to discuss techniques.

There was also a strong religious influence to everyday life, and each day began with a visit to the Chapel at 6.00 a.m. In this and all other aspects of school life discipline was strict and the requirement to take and pass exams dominant. Nevertheless, Montague survived this draconian environment, and indeed flourished in it.

The first indications of Montague's interest in a legal career may have been seen in his debating talent. He was Secretary of the college debating society and spoke on such political and social issues as the merits of the French Revolution, the dangers of Bismarck's influence on Europe, which he described as 'morally and socially a curse', and the relationship between Man and State. He also spoke against slavery and the subjugation of women. He supported fashion as a mixture of beauty and utility and hailed Wordsworth as an example of Protestantism. Clearly he was that unusual combination of the sporting, the cultural and the academic with his own view of the future. In 1876 his peers recognised this, and he became the Prefect of Chapel.

Like generations of schoolboys before and after him, Montague wished to leave his mark on the school, literally. But not for him a name scratched on a classroom desk or a dining room table: Montague with a certain vandalistic style chose the centuries-old oak panelling of School. His name remains there to this day, engraved to the left of the fireplace on the south wall. If it was a small attempt at immortality, he need not have bothered as a greater and even less meritorious route awaited him. The name Montague Druitt still creates interest among the boys of Winchester. He has a chapter in a Wykehamist publication about unusual former pupils, and the place in the dormitory where his bed stood is still known. E.B. Noel's book on Winchester College Cricket details all those up to 1926 who played in the 1st XI and so could be included in the honoured list of Lord's Men. Montague's name is among them.

The progression of someone of Montague's talents and popularity to Oxford or Cambridge was natural. After taking preliminary examinations in 1875, he won a scholarship to New College, Oxford, the following year. This was predictable, since both Winchester and New College were founded by Bishop William of Wykeham – the school in 1382 and the College in 1379. From then until 1856 Winchester was the feeder school for New College, and for nearly five centuries supplied most of New College's undergraduates. Nor did the new undergraduates have to be scholars. Patronage and social connections were widely used, and boys might be allocated places at New College at the age of 13, which scarcely encouraged them to concentrate on examinations. There was also the absurd Founder's Kin method of entry based on the legend that some descendants of the Founder had killed themselves at St Mary's College in the late sixteenth century. The result was that thirty-one boys from Winchester were allowed to claim Founder's Kin. The entry test was simple. The applicant was hit ceremonially on the head with a stick, and if the stick broke he was accepted. Not surprisingly, by the 1850s academic standards at the college were poor, and a number of reforms were put in place, including the abolition of the Founder's Kin. By the time Montague entered New College in 1876, intellectual standards were much better and his scholarship in Classics was a legitimate achievement.

FOUR

'Very nice sort of place, Oxford'

At the time of Montague's arrival in October 1876, New College had no great reputation for encouraging sport. Perhaps the drive for better academic standards over the previous twenty years had precluded this. At about this time a man named Hastings Rashdall held much influence over the college. He was an architectural historian and moral philosopher who strongly disliked the emphasis on sport in English public schools. Rashdall's views had the support of his teaching colleagues, so when Montague arrived his athletic skills cut little ice. He was not a single-minded academic, so he would not have been picked out for the best teaching, nor would he have been encouraged by the Warden of New College, John Edwards Sewell. Sewell became Warden in 1860 at the age of 50 and remained in office until he died at 92. Known as 'the Shirt', he preferred to carry out antiquarian research and build up the college archives. His vision was strictly backward, and any progress the college made during his term was not of his making. His most memorable act was to have clothes painted onto Biagio Rebecca's nude figures of Adam and Eve on one of the north windows of the chapel. At best he was a symbol of continuity. It is safe to say Montague would not have been his favourite person, and vice versa.

Nevertheless Montague was not deterred from his love of sport. In 1877 he won the university double Fives and the single Fives, and he played rugby for his college. He also made an impressive impact on the Freshmen's Match. In the opposing side was the Etonian Evelyn Ruggles-Brise. Montague bowled him out cheaply in both innings. Ruggles-Brise would not have forgotten this disappointment, nor the name Montague Druitt, and the memory of those dismissals would have been even more galling when his younger brother Harold, a Wykehamist, won a Blue for Oxford a few years later. Who knows how it might have influenced his attitude to Montague later on. Ruggles-Brise did not appear in senior university cricket again. Montague took 6 wickets in the match, but this was not enough to get him into the Oxford XI. However, his talent did continue to command respect, and in 1880 he played in the Seniors' Match for C.E. Horner's side, and took 3 wickets. For some reason Montague played only on the first day, after which he was marked 'absent'. In the opposition side, led by Robert Knight, was William Patterson, who captained Kent and became President of the county. After Oxford, Patterson and Montague continued to meet on the cricket field.

Unfortunately, during Montague's four years at Oxford he was in competition for the fast bowling places with the likes of Alfred Evans, Walter Thornton and Norman MacLachlan. They all went on to play first-class cricket. But his inability to break into the very top of university cricket did not discourage him, and for the three seasons 1877–9 he played in most of the New College matches and was a consistent wicket-taker. The records for his last year, 1880, have been lost, but there is no reason to suppose he did not continue just as keenly. In the season of 1879 (and perhaps 1880) he was the Cricket Secretary for the college, and this must have eroded his time for study. As a man who saw the value of university life in a broader perspective than merely the chasing of exam results he was ahead of his time. On the cricket field, at least, he was honing his skills for what was really the love of his short life.

At Oxford Montague met up with the Webbe brothers. He and Herbert were both at New College and regularly played in the college team. Herbert, however, was a very good player and won three Blues. He and his brother, Alexander, formed a formidable opening partnership. To this day they are the only brothers to have opened the innings in the Varsity Match, which they achieved twice, at Lord's in 1877 and 1878. Alexander Webbe went on to play for England and toured Australia with Lord Harris's side. The brothers did share one embarrassing cricketing moment when, in May 1877, the Oxford side including the brothers was dismissed by MCC for 12. Alexander arrived two hours late, and by the time he did so the innings was over. In the second innings Oxford amassed 35. It did not matter. A few weeks later Oxford, led by Alexander, easily won the Varsity Match.

Through cricket at Oxford in the late 1870s, Montague would have known Harold Christopherson, who played regularly as a teenager for his father's side, the Christopherson Brothers. The team consisted of the father and his ten sons, and it played matches mostly against Blackheath Cricket Club from 1877–91, with one break. Harold Christopherson was to prove to be a most significant contact when later Montague left Oxford and was seeking employment.

It was also at Oxford that Montague became friends with a fellow undergraduate, Reginald Brodie Dyke Acland. The two played Fives and cricket together. Reginald was the son of Sir Henry Acland, the Honorary Physician to the Prince of Wales, later Edward VII, and a great friend of Sir William Gull. It is thought it was Sir Henry who introduced Gull to royal circles. Gull became doctor to Queen Victoria, and was implicated in the scandals involving the royal family and the five Whitechapel murders. Montague would have met Henry Acland, and quite probably William Gull.

Although they were not contemporaries at Oxford, Montague later got to know Trevitt Hine-Haycock when playing in the early 1880s for the Incogniti Cricket Club. Hine-Haycock was part of the family that for years was the cornerstone of Sidmouth cricket, and he was an excellent player. He won two Blues, played for Kent and toured

North America. In a match at Sidmouth in 1881 Montague caught and bowled him for 0. However, Hine-Haycock's great claim to fame was to be a member of the Oxford side that defeated the touring Australians in 1884. It is a feat no Oxford team has ever repeated. In the first innings the formidable Frederick Spofforth disposed of Hine-Haycock quickly. In the second innings Oxford needed 108 runs to win, but lost 3 early wickets. However Hine-Haycock and Manley Kemp added an unbroken 80 and the match was won. Hine-Haycock's elation as he walked back to the pavilion with the defeated Australians trailing in behind can hardly be imagined. From that moment he must have been convinced there was a God in heaven. At any rate he entered the Church, was ordained in 1890, and served as Priest in Ordinary to the King for twenty-six years.

Hine-Haycock also went to New College, where he remains revered: the only cricketer mentioned by name in *New College Oxford 1379–1979*. That this book omits Douglas Jardine, another New College man and one of the most interesting and controversial cricketers who ever lived, is another indication of Hine-Haycock's status. In the late 1920s Douglas Jardine followed in Montague's footsteps from Winchester to New College, and like Montague spent much of his time playing cricket. He never forgot his allegiance to Oxford cricket, and, even when playing for England, he wore his Harlequin cap. Jardine achieved permanent fame and notoriety for conceiving the idea of 'Bodyline' bowling. He was appointed captain of the England cricket team for the tour of Australia 1932–3, which he knew would be extremely difficult. His plan was simple. He had two very quick fast bowlers, Harold Larwood and Bill Voce, backed up by 'Gubby' Allen and Bill Bowes, and he instructed them (Larwood and Voce, in particular) to bowl fast, short-pitched balls at the batsmen's ribs. Several Australians were hit and carried off as they simply could not address such intimidating bowling. Even Bradman had his average halved. The Australian press were furious, and the Australian Cricket Board complained to the MCC and threatened to curtail the tour. The MCC establishment, though, was stoutly behind Jardine. 'Plum' Warner, the tour manager later to be knighted for his services, was happy, and the MCC committee supported him with the reply to the ACB: 'We at Marylebone Cricket Club deplore your cable. We deprecate your opinion that there has been unsportsmanlike play. We have fullest confidence in captain, team, and manager.'

The Australian government became nervous and, fearing a loss of trade if the tour was cancelled, instructed the ACB to withdraw from the argument. The tour was completed and ended in a 4–1 series win for England. But the controversy has never been forgotten nor forgiven, and a whole procession of Australian fast bowlers from Ray Lindwall to Glenn McGrath have been redressing the score ever since. It was Rockley Wilson, another Wykehamist, who saw the row coming. He was a good player for England and Yorkshire and had returned to Winchester, where he taught the young Jardine. He was therefore well equipped to make the comment on Jardine's appointment: 'We shall win the Ashes, but we may lose a dominion.'

The MCC's support did not last long. Despite winning two further series against the West Indies and India, the authorities lost confidence and sacked Jardine the following year. This was described by Simon Wilde in the *Sunday Times* as 'the greatest betrayal of a captain'. Jardine's omission from the book about Montague's old college is therefore strange.

The New College book is a serious work with some good anecdotes buried among references to Thomas Aquinas and the Venerable Bede. It shows clearly that not all students were financially secure as in the eighteenth century two of them supplemented their grants by setting themselves up as highwaymen. It was not their vocation. They were caught and hanged at 'Gownsmen's Gallows' in Holywell, the area adjacent to New College. Most probably they were also Wykehamists.

Another tale involves John Woodforde who, with a BA and the status of a Fellow of the College safely tucked away, eschewed intellectual concerns and concentrated on 'cricket, bowls and billiards' together with a generous alcohol intake. As he said, 'I carried off my drinking exceedingly well indeed.' The book exonerates him, because he liked music, attended concerts and played the harpsichord.

The suggestion that Montague was not really encouraged in his cricket activities is borne out by the reason why the university moved the cricket ground away from Cowley Marsh and nearer to Oxford. This was not for the benefit of the players but to reduce vandalism on the roads and to lessen the level of drunkeness at the post-match parties. More prosaic may have been the match in 1930 when the New College choristers visited King's College Cambridge for a match against their counterparts. They lost the match but no doubt enjoyed singing Evensong in King's Chapel.

There was another New College cricket team during Montague's time at Oxford. It was called 'The Snarks' and was named to celebrate the publication in 1876 of Lewis Carroll's (the pseudonym of Charles Dodgson) lengthy nonsense poem, *The Hunting of the Snark*. Dodgson had been at Oxford some twenty years earlier. It was not a serious team, and frequently played with less than 11-a-side. It would not have appealed to Montague, but later in 1882 his brother Arthur played a few times. It is the only record of Arthur's involvement in cricket.

Montague was not a one-dimensional, purely academic student, and unfortunately it showed when, on 10 July 1880, he was awarded a Third Class degree in Classics. Any student would be disappointed with a Third, but to someone of Montague's obvious ability it was a serious setback. Even today both Winchester and New College regard his time at Oxford as a failure. They ignore the amount he contributed to college life by his debating and sporting activities; he was also elected Steward of the Junior Common room by his peers, which would reinforce the view that he was a popular and well-balanced personality.

A letter that survives from his Oxford days indicates a shrewd ability to handle people appropriately. Montague wrote it to his uncle Robert soon after he went up to New College. He obviously viewed Robert with much respect, even awe, and he set out to create an impression of earnest application to his studies. He discusses the grammatical merits of a piece of Vergil translation, the use of the indefinite article, and gives a rather superior critique of cousin Kitty's technical knowledge of Latin. The tone of the letter makes it clear that he regarded the approval of Uncle Robert, himself a well-known and innovative doctor, as very important. He signed the letter, most dutifully 'Your affectionate nephew M.J. Druitt'. Perhaps it was this ability that led him to be so easily accepted by people such as Lord Harris later on.

His lack of exam success may be put down to his extramural interests, and they certainly did absorb much of his time, but it is also likely he simply lost interest in his chosen subjects of Latin and Greek. His debating talent suggests he was more suited for the Law, in which he eventually qualified. His mistake was possibly not to use his Classics achievements at Winchester to enter Oxford and then to change his subject of study. Nevertheless, despite his exam results, Montague would have fully agreed with George Bernard Shaw's comment: 'Very nice sort of place, Oxford.'

FIVE

To Work, Rest and Play

When Montague returned home from Oxford in the summer of 1880 he cannot have looked forward to meeting his father. After ten years of the best education England had to offer, he carried with him a Third Class degree. By now William, his elder brother, was a solicitor, and Montague was expected to be something equally professional and respectable. Montague devised a plan that required all his debating skills to sell to his father. He suggested that the decision to do Classics instead of Law at Oxford was a mistake, and Law was his true vocation; many of his colleagues at New College were becoming barristers, and with his effectiveness in arguing and debating and a sharp and lively mind he was a natural. His father, however, was reluctant to finance him any further. There were four more children after Montague to be educated, and a household of Westfield's size with the obligatory servants was not cheap to run.

Montague had anticipated this response and made two suggestions. He would take a teaching job within easy distance of London's Lincoln's Inn Fields, the centre of law teaching and practices, which would give him financial independence, and he would be able at the same time to follow the appropriate studies. Montague could argue that there was nothing demeaning for a Wykehamist to have a career that did not bring immediate prosperity. Traditionally Wykehamists either entered the Church or taught in Grammar schools to meet the growing demand for literacy, so Montague could have claimed he was a throwback to the sixteenth century, an argument his conservative father might have liked. Montague knew that even to study at the Inns of Court would be expensive. There was the large admission fee to pay, and, as part of the tradition, dozens of dinners had to be taken in Hall over three years. These were costly and the wine bill substantial. Then there were the fees for sitting the examinations and finally, when he was qualified, there was the Bar Call fee. Montague had the answer to these financial problems. He proposed to his father that his share of any future inheritance should be brought forward and he would forfeit any future financial prospects. William Druitt was sufficiently convinced by the plan to advance £500 allocated in his will, and the way was clear for Montague to enter the Inns of Court.

His argument had been plausible and to an extent honest, as he genuinely wished to study Law. But there was one large element of his plan that may not have been discussed – Montague wanted to play lots of cricket. It is likely that even before he had gained his father's approval for the plan, Montague had a job lined up. At Oxford he had known Harold Christopherson, and he would have learnt about the Christopherson family team and their close connection with Blackheath Morden Cricket Club. He would have realised, if he did not know already, that Blackheath was one of the strongest and most prestigious clubs in England. Harold might also have told him that a George Valentine, a member of the club, was the headmaster of a small, successful boys' school nearby, and one of the staff, Frederick Lacey, was also a Blackheath member. Blackheath was, of course, extremely convenient for Lincoln's Inn Fields.

The other reason why Montague would have chosen to move to Blackheath was because of a man he must have known in Wimborne, Nicholas Felix. It is possible that Felix may have been the biggest influence on young Montague's life outside his family.

Nicholas Felix was born in 1804 in Camberwell and took over running a local school at the age of 19 when his father, the headmaster, died suddenly. In 1832 he moved the school, called Alfred House, to Blackheath and was able to combine schoolmastering with playing cricket for Kent. Felix was a cricketer first and schoolmaster second. It was noticed that Alfred House as a school had declined to a stage where there remained only eleven pupils, but when questioned about this Felix replied, 'True, but if I have only eleven boys, they shall play any other eleven boys in England.' It seems these stories reached Montague and he remembered them.

Felix was of Belgian descent. His real name was Wanostrocht, but, as he was concerned that the parents of his pupils would not approve of his cricket activities (since cricket was then somewhat associated with gambling), he adopted the 'nom de cricket' Felix, a name he always preferred. Not only did Felix become one of the best players of the mid-nineteenth century, but while at Blackheath he invented in 1837 a bowling machine called the 'catapulta', after a Roman military weapon. The basic design continued to be used for the rest of the century. The original was a fairly crude iron affair made by the local blacksmith, and Felix eventually gave the machine to a friend of his at Blackheath, John Spencer. Felix's other invention was the tubular India rubber batting gloves. Felix was a member of Blackheath Dartmouth Cricket Club, a 'sister' club of Blackheath Morden, and had been watching cricket on the Heath since it began in the 1820s. He was an excellent artist and produced many watercolours of leading players of the era such as Fuller Pitch and Walter Mynn. His painting of William Clarke's All England XI of 1847, which included himself, still hangs in the pavilion at Lord's. Much of his enthusiasm and skill in painting can be traced to the great Victorian artist George Frederick Watts, who was a pupil at Felix's school. Watts became known as 'England's Michelangelo', and when Felix wrote his classic instruction book *Felix on the Bat*, Watts provided the illustrations.

All this would become significant when, in 1845, Felix began visiting Wimborne regularly, as the arrival of a person of his fame would have had an impact on a small town. Eventually in 1872 Felix with his second wife moved to Wimborne, where he continued to teach cricket to the local boys in the field beside his house. In 1872 Montague would have been 15, and a combination of Felix's reputation and the standing of Montague's own family make it almost certain that he would have received tuition from the great man. Apart from the coaching, Montague would have been fascinated by such an interesting and multi-talented person. He would have listened to stories of the match in Felix's honour at Lord's in June 1846 when the Felix XI played the Fuller Pitch XI, a game that was attended by Prince Albert, who arrived on a horse. He would also have heard accounts of cricket at Blackheath.

Felix was an amusing, generous man who loved music and studied the classics and for Montague he must have been like a breath of fresh air. Here was a relaxed friendly adult telling him tales that can only have stimulated Montague and opened his eyes to another world. Until to then he had led a rather repressed life, and may have thought that the whole adult world shared the philosophies of his father, George Ridding and later John Sewell. Felix had unwittingly given him a new and far more interesting view of life, and perhaps it was a vision he never forgot.

Felix continued to paint in retirement in Wimborne. Even when he lost the use of his right hand through paralysis, he managed to paint a small self-portrait with his left, and sent it to his old friend Lord Bessborough. Bessborough described him as 'one of the cleverest, most accomplished, kind hearted and truest friends I ever had'. When Felix died in Wimborne in 1876, *Wisden* carried an obituary notice: 'Mr Felix (Mr Nicholas Wanostrocht) an accomplished cricketer, artist, musician and gentleman.' He was buried in the local cemetery, and just thirteen years later Montague was to join him.

Blackheath seemed to attract the innovative spirit. The advent of the train in the mid-nineteenth century had greatly facilitated travel to away cricket matches, but reaching smaller places with no station remained a problem. It was the cricketers of Blackheath who around 1900 first noted the arrival of the bicycle. They realised that pads and bat could be tied to the crossbar and more remote grounds reached. In the 1960s George Hughes-Games, a member of the Incogniti, took the idea a stage further. He managed to tie on a tent as well, and so succeeded in becoming free of public transport and overnight accommodation. He would cover the team's West Country tour by bicycle, and set up camp near the opposition's pavilion. He was accompanied by his pointer, Bede, who travelled in the front basket.

So it was not by chance that Montague ended up in Blackheath. At Oxford Harold Christopherson would have enjoyed the stories of Nicholas Felix, and added his own enthusiasm for Blackheath. This would have been in the summer of 1880, as Montague was finishing at New College and considering his plans for the future. It is perfectly possible that Harold recounted these conversations to his family, who were friends and club mates of George Valentine at Blackheath. A player of Montague's ability, from a very respectable family with a good social demeanour and an excellent education would be attractive to the club. So it was to everyone's advantage when George Valentine had a vacancy for an assistant master. Montague was promptly appointed in time for the autumn term in 1880.

George Valentine had opened the school under his name in 1873. Its purpose was to train boys to go on to public schools and universities, and eventually to take up military or professional careers. The age range of the boys was 9–17, and the school's capacity about forty. It appears to have been successful and well run, and several of the boys later appeared in *Who's Who*. However, the claim that Benjamin Disraeli, twice British Prime Minister, was a former pupil of George Valentine's school is not true. When Valentine opened his school in 1873, Disraeli was 69! There is a link, which is the basis of the myth. Four owners, several name changes and a change of address earlier, there was a school down the road at 2 & 3 Eliot Place. It was run by the Nonconformist minister Revd John Potticary, and Disraeli attended this school for three years from 1814. Disraeli was Jewish, but the school was liberal in politics and religion, and he received instruction from a rabbi who came to the school once a week.

Prior to George Valentine the owner of the school at 9 Eliot Place was the Revd Thomas Nunn. He tired of Blackheath and started a new school in Maidenhead called St Piran's. It still exists today. The owner before Nunn had been the Revd Richard Powles and he had left an unusual legacy: a swimming pool, which he had had installed in about 1860 and which was still there in Montague's time. Montague was a good swimmer and would have enjoyed this facility. Contemporary accounts from former pupils and masters suggest the school was quite large – it was set in six acres. The basement housed the dining hall. At ground level the schoolroom was divided into two classrooms, and above it was a large room for daytime activities. On the next floor were the dormitories, and finally at the top was the masters' common room, complete with a piano. It was therefore a substantial property on five floors, and with ample grounds for sports. These playing fields were referred to by a resident as 'the green which Mr Valentine tends so ably with water and roller'. This suggests the school had a cricket pitch, again a facility of great interest to Montague, and one that offered him an opportunity for coaching.

There were two or three assistant masters. One of these was Frederick Lacey, also a keen member of Blackheath Morden and five years older than Montague. He did not sleep overnight at the school, as it is known he had lodgings down the road at Lee with a nurseryman called George Saville. By 1881 a third master, Mark Mann, had joined the staff. This may have indicated the school was doing well and expanding. There were also ten other members of staff, including a housekeeper, a matron, a cook, housemaids and several servants.

Little is known of Montague's day-to-day responsibilities at the school, and perhaps there were not too many. He could well have been employed on the understanding that he was intending a legal career and would therefore need time to study, and that his housemaster duties should not interfere with his cricket. It has been suggested the Montague's main role was the night-time master. He always slept at the school during term time, and he gave 9 Eliot Place as his home address. Frederick Lacey, we know, lived away from the school, and from 1885 so too did Valentine. When his mother died at the end of that year, Valentine went to live in her house at 97 Dacre Park. This was a short distance from the school, but it meant that Montague was almost certainly the night master in charge, and would have remained so for the rest of his time at the school. If his job was something of a sinecure, it could be another explanation for the appointment of Mark Mann.

It took no time for Montague to be elected into Blackheath Morden Cricket Club. He was proposed by George Valentine, whose brother William happened to be on the Committee, and seconded by Frederick Lacey. With the support of the Christopherson family and his own good credentials, his election was a formality. Montague made the transition from university cricket to club cricket with ease. In his first season with Blackheath he took 32 wickets, which put him third in the list of wicket-takers behind Frederick Ireland, another Kent player, and ahead of Stanley Christopherson. The next year he was elected onto the Committee, a sure sign of the respect his colleagues had developed for him in a short time. Moreover, he was made Treasurer. At the time Sir C.H. Mills, the local MP, was the President, and William Valentine and Frederick Lacey were both fellow Committee members. The captain, Frederick Prior, a wealthy stockbroker and one of the most important figures in Blackheath history, had, since the 1860s, built the club into its dominating position.

In 1882 Montague's efforts towards a legal career bore some success. He was admitted to the Inner Temple and he was thus on his way to achieving his ambition of becoming a barrister. This, together with a growing reputation at Blackheath and an undemanding job, meant that Montague was enjoying life. His only problem may have been money. As a schoolmaster he would not have been making more than £200 a year, less board and lodging at the school. His cricketing adventures, which extended outside Blackheath, had to be paid for. His legal fees and subscriptions were also a drain. Nevertheless, with the help of his father he showed no sign of compromising his lifestyle.

The one sadness in this year for Montague was the death, aged 21, of Harold Christopherson. Harold was an undergraduate at

Oxford and was earning some holiday money as a tutor to the family of Viscount Studley at Wakehurst Place, Ardingly. On 21 September he was out riding in the park with the Viscount's three children, and was seen to be passing under some low branches at a gallop. Harold did not duck low enough and took a heavy fall. A coachman carried Harold, unconscious, back to the house and the doctor was called. It was to no avail. Harold died later the same day and the coroner's diagnosis was that the 'cause of death was concussion of the brain and fracture of the base of the skull'. His death devastated the Christopherson family. He was the eldest son and a model to his nine brothers and sister. The Blackheath community, especially the cricket club, was also shocked. It was a sad blow to Montague, as it does seem that Harold had been instrumental in bringing him to Blackheath. After a year's break in their fixtures, the Christophersons resumed playing as a team but now always fielded ten: the father plus the nine surviving sons.

For a man in an increasingly secure social position with an impressive list of acquaintances gained mostly through cricket, it was natural that Montague would wish to join the MCC. Again his referees were impeccable. He was proposed by Charles Seymour, a Harrovian, barrister and a player for MCC and Hampshire who later became a Justice of the Peace for Wiltshire and Hampshire. His seconder was the Revd Vernon Royle. He won two Blues at Oxford, went with Lord Harris's side to Australia in 1878 and played in the Melbourne Test. In 1929 he became President of Lancashire Cricket Club. When he seconded Montague he was a schoolmaster in Elstree. Montague was now becoming well known and popular in cricket circles. He gained priority membership into MCC as a 'cricketer' and was duly elected on 26 May 1884. He was now able to rub shoulders with half of England's gentry in the Lord's pavilion.

Montague's MCC membership came through just in time for him to be eligible to watch, from the exclusivity of the pavilion, one of Blackheath Cricket Club's proudest moments. Stanley Christopherson, for several years an active member, had been chosen to play for England against Australia in the inaugural Test Match at Lord's. Montague's feelings must have been of great pride. A man with whom he had often opened the bowling at Blackheath was playing for England alongside ten of the most famous players of his generation, and in some cases in the history of the game. The side is worth recalling:

> W.G. Grace
> A.P. Lucas
> Arthur Shrewsbury
> George Ulyett
> A.G. Steel
> Lord Harris
> R.G. Barlow
> W.W. Read
> Hon. Alfred Lyttleton
> Edmund Peate
> Stanley Christopherson

Montague was a member of the world's most prestigious club, and he would have delighted in the excitement of seeing a colleague and friend perform at the pinnacle of international cricket. By association he shared Christopherson's achievement. Christopherson did not disappoint. He had the giant George Bonner caught by Grace at cover and made 17 runs. Then Peate and Ulyett (who took 13 wickets between them) destroyed Australia, and England won by an innings.

It was a fine year for Montague. Not only did he top the list of Blackheath wicket-takers and was appointed club Secretary – a position he had held at Oxford for New College – but in July he passed the Intermediate Law Examination and the following November he passed the General Examination. He was closer to fulfilling his ambition to become a barrister.

SIX

'Modest merit but slowly makes its way'

Although Montague had another successful season with Blackheath Cricket Club in 1885, the undoubted highlight occurred on 29 April when he passed his final Law exams and was called to the Bar of the Inner Temple. *The Times* recorded the event. This was a vindication of the plan he had put to his father five years earlier. He had succeeded and was a barrister. With the help of his father's £500 in advance of his inheritance and his work at the school, he had made financial ends meet, and played endless cricket. Straightaway, he rented chambers at 9 King's Bench Walk in the Inner Temple, putting himself alongside the cream of England's legal profession. His father must have been extremely proud.

Today, 9 King's Bench Walk stands much as it did more than a century ago, a part of a fine five-storey Georgian terrace overlooking the elegant railed gardens of the Inner Temple. The area exudes a hushed, affluent solemnity. After an education at Winchester and Oxford, Montague would have been at ease in such surroundings. The rental for his chambers would have been about £60 a year – quite a slice out of his schoolmaster's salary. However, he joined the Western Circuit and Winchester Sessions and looked forward to business.

On the cricket field he flourished. His 41 wickets for Blackheath were exceeded only by Stanley Christopherson, and his 331 runs included a 76 not out. It was a score he exceeded only twice, both times in 1883 – firstly 82 not out for Blackheath against the Royal Naval College, then 83 not out for George Valentine's school against Blackheath. In the club report for year 1885 he received the tribute: 'Mr M.J. Druitt takes the Bat with an average of 33.1 in 13 innings.' Bats were awarded at the end of each season to the players with the best overall performances for batting and bowling, and for any special individual effort such as a hat-trick. Within the club it was an honour to receive a Bat. This award was remarkable considering Montague was primarily a bowler.

Off the field a further distinction had come his way when, in early 1885, the club was reconstituted. This became necessary as Blackheath Morden had to give up playing on the Heath, so Montague as Secretary and Arthur Poland, the Treasurer, asked the rugby club if the cricket club could share the rugby club's ground at Rectory Field. This was agreed, and the Blackheath Cricket, Football and Lawn Tennis Company was formed. Montague became one of the three cricket directors for the new company. The fact he had a top professional qualification would certainly have helped him, as now he could present himself as a barrister. His co-directors were Frederick Prior and Frederick Ireland, a solicitor. At the same time Dr Lennard Stokes, captain of England's rugby team, was on the General Committee. The first meeting of the directors of the new club took place at Lincoln's Inn Fields on 11 June 1885. Of the initial share issue Montague bought five and acquired two more later on.

Throughout Montague's time at Blackheath two families in particular had influenced his career and his cricket. They were the Valentines and the Christophersons. It was Harold Christopherson who originally encouraged him to go to Blackheath, and once there it was George Valentine who employed him, and helped him join the cricket club. In the 1880s the Valentines – especially George and his brother William – were keen supporters of the club, although it could be said that William's main contribution to Kent cricket was through his grandson, Bryan Herbert Valentine. Born in 1908, he played seven times for England, scored two centuries, made 18,000 runs for Kent and became their Secretary and President. The Valentine connection with Kent cricket continues to this day. Bryan's son, Errol, is the Fixture Secretary for the Kent League, and the godfather of May, Bryan's daughter, is Colin Ingleby-McKenzie, whose exuberant leadership took Hampshire to their first county championship title win in 1961.

With so many Christopherson and Valentine offspring based in the Blackheath area, it was not surprising that the two families became linked by marriage. In 1902 a Christopherson daughter, Catherine, married another George Valentine, and a few years later Louisa Valentine married a Henry Christopherson. Montague therefore lived through a very important period of Blackheath cricket history, and was extremely close to two of its most significant families.

Soon after the end of the 1885 season, there was a setback in Montague's happy and successful life. On 27 September his father, William, died suddenly. William Druitt, a devout churchgoer, had been looking forward to the celebration of the harvest festival at Wimborne Minster that Sunday evening. He had had a history of heart problems and had stopped practising as a doctor a few years earlier. However, it was completely unexpected when at midday he collapsed and died within minutes. His funeral on the following Thursday at the Minster was impressive. It was meant to be private, but many of the town's principal inhabitants and tradespeople joined the family. The service was conducted by five vicars. The organist played 'The Dead March' from *Saul*, the choir sang 'Now the labourer's task is o'er' and the muffled peals of the Minster bells rang out over Wimborne. William Druitt was a highly respected man, a pillar of the community. He was 65, and he joined Nicholas Felix in the Minster's cemetery.

It is possible that Montague was saddened but not devastated by the loss. From the personal opinions gleaned from his debating record he seems more broad-minded and forward-looking than his father. William Druitt's will bore out his careful nature. His estate was valued at £16,579, well over half a million pounds today, and Montague's share was £500, but, since this amount had already been advanced, there was no more money to come. However, Montague did receive all his father's pictures, books, clocks, jewellery and ornaments, which could well have had a significant value as a family of the Druitts' status living in style in a handsome estate would have had some major pictures.

There was indeed an indication that there were pictures and that they had a very real value. In 1841 a Captain Druitt, who would have been of the same generation as Montague's grandmother, sold a collection of wonderful pictures at Christie's in London. There were sixty-eight paintings, chiefly the work of the Italian, Spanish and Flemish masters including Rubens, Teniers, Rembrandt, Van Dyck, Murillo, Caravaggio and Titian. All but seven sold, but, of these, three were by Murillo, plus a Rosa, a Caravaggio, a Raffaello and Rubens's *Suzannah and the Elders*. If these were returned to the family (and perhaps there were others not put up for sale), then Montague's inheritance, over forty years later, would have been substantial. It would explain how Montague managed to leave an estate of nearly £1,500 when he died. Even so, Montague may have felt a little disappointed by the absence of any cash lump sum in his father's will. He knew that his father had advanced him the £500 inheritance five years before, but perhaps he had hoped for a little more generosity.

It was normal practice at the time for wealthy fathers to pay for the education of their sons, usually at public school and then at university, but Montague had achieved scholarships to Winchester (except for the first two terms) and to Oxford, so his father's fees and expenses would have been low. Nevertheless, he was not prepared to fund Montague's legal education. The eldest brother, William, inherited a farm at Child Okeford in Dorset, and the three daughters each received £6,000 providing they did not marry before the age of 21. The bequests therefore exceeded the value of the estate. In William Druitt's defence there was a Victorian egalitarianism in this distribution. Money may not have been spent on their education, but the daughters were generously provided for to help them marry well and to enable them to offer a substantial dowry. Montague's mother, Ann, received 'rents, income, wine, coal and corn'. It is not possible to evaluate this legacy, but it was sufficient. When Ann died in 1890 she left a respectable £2,400.

It was Ann who was most affected by her husband's death. Almost at once her health and mental stability began to decline, and family life for the Druitts at Westfield House was never the same again.

Montague's prowess on the cricket field was not affected by his father's death. The 1886 season started promptly with a celebration match on 26 April against G.G. Hearne's XI. It marked the opening of the new ground at Rectory Field, a project to which Montague had contributed a great deal. It is still the home of Blackheath cricket. The Hearne side included six of the famous Hearne family. The match also marked the arrival of a groundsman, George Street, and his wife Louisa, who helped with the catering and worked behind the bar. It was she who pulled the first pint to celebrate the new ground. The position of groundsman was then passed from father to son within the Street family until 1963 – a dynasty that lasted four generations. At first George Street had been turned down for the post. Remarkably, Street's original letter of application still exists, as does the Secretary's reply rejecting him. The Secretary was, of course, Montague, and his note is one of only two known original letters that survive from his hand. But Street persevered and a few weeks later he was appointed in time for the new season.

The following June Montague had perhaps the best cricket month of his life. On the 5th he played against the Band of Brothers, a very strong wandering Kent side, which included Lord Harris and several of the Kent 1st XI. Montague made 41, and had the effrontery to bowl the noble Lord for 14. He then accounted for John Tonge, William Patterson and Richard Jones, all good Kent batsmen. At this stage Montague must have been close to getting a game for Kent, but the call never came. The next week he faced the Incogniti, and the following Saturday he clean bowled the England opener, and long-time Surrey captain, John Shuter for 0. This proved to be

Montague's best season – 370 runs and top wicket-taker with 50. His efforts were officially recognised by an entry in the 1886 Annual Report: 'Mr Druitt and Mr Cruikshank have also bowled extremely well throughout the season.' This year the coveted Bat for bowling went to Sidney Christopherson.

However, his legal career was not doing so well, although in May, in his role as a special pleader at the Middlesex Sheriff's Court, he had a success that was recorded in the national press. His client, Miss Marion Mildon, won damages for a breach of promise of marriage, and the jury, under Montague's persuasion, awarded her £50, but by the end of 1886 Montague had still received no full briefs despite being registered with the Western Circuit and the Winchester Sessions. This failure was not altogether surprising. It was estimated at the time that fewer than one in eight barristers ever received a brief, and a contemporary, George Sims the dramatist, noted: 'The life of men who have come enthusiastic to the law and have utterly failed would fill as many pages as are contained in a complete set of law reports.'

The author John Wilding discovered a piece written by C.W. Heckthorn in *London Souvenirs* in 1899:

Success at the Bar comes to barristers in the most capricious manner. In this profession as in many other pursuits, modest merit but slowly makes its way. Manners maketh the man, but impudence an advocate; without this latter quality even high connections and powerful patronage often seems ineffectual. Earl Camden, son of Chief Justice Pratt was called to the Bar in his twenty-fourth year and remained a briefless barrister for nine long years when he resolved to abandon Westminster Hall for his College Fellowship.

If it was so difficult for a barrister to succeed, why was the legal profession not more selective in accepting students and their fees? The legal education fees were about £500, so, for every 100 unsuccessful barristers, £50,000 was being collected. In today's values this would be approaching £3 million.

Montague did earn some money from his qualifications. The Law List for 1887 describes him as a special pleader for the Western Circuit for Hampshire, Portsmouth and Southampton Assizes. This fairly junior work involved putting together an argument on behalf of the plaintiff to demonstrate the extent to which he or she had suffered by the defendant's actions. Alternatively, pleas could be entered on behalf of the defendant to argue for his or her discharge from prosecution. Pleadings were usually written statements delivered to the judges' chambers, and were not discussed in open court. Special pleaders no longer exist, but in their time the work was usually carried out by law students not yet called to the Bar. It was not a well-paid, or prestigious task for Montague, but it earned him something to supplement his modest schoolmaster's salary. The work also allowed him to retain his chambers in King's Bench Walk. Had he been completely inactive he would have been asked to leave. Many 'dormant' barristers tried to maintain their chambers for reasons of prestige, or for the convenience of a London residence. Even as a special pleader he was senior enough to be invited to attend a dinner given by members of the Western Circuit in November to mark the promotion of Mr Justice Charles to the Bench.

There is evidence in the pattern of matches that he played for Blackheath that summer that Montague was taking his special-pleading work seriously. Up to 25 July he played nearly every weekend and sometimes mid-week. After that he did not play again that season. As 25 July was about the end of the school term, it seems likely that he then returned to the West Country, where his legal work was centred. A further reason for his return to the area was the worsening condition of his mother. By now Ann Druitt had delusions she was being electrocuted, had suicidal tendencies and would not spend money or eat. She was exhibiting the symptoms of clinical depression. This was alarming, as her own mother had also had mental difficulties and had committed suicide. Many years later Georgiana, Montague's eldest sister, killed herself by jumping from a top-floor window.

Living in the West Country, Montague was still well able to continue his cricket. For years he had played occasionally for Canford Manor, Bournemouth and Kingston Park, and these strong clubs would have been glad to give him a game. Canford Manor was Lord Wimborne's own team and ground, and no doubt Montague's regular appearances underpinned the friendship that existed between the two families.

Up to July his season at Blackheath had been busy and successful. His most memorable match was against Surrey Club and Ground in May, when he bowled Robert Abel for 56. Abel was a prolific scorer for England and Surrey. He toured Australia and South Africa and in 1900 broke W.G. Grace's record for scoring twelve first-class hundreds in a single season. In the same match the scorer in his book makes a special note of an even bigger prize that just eluded Montague: 'M.J. Druitt bowled W.W. Read with a no ball before he had scored.' Read, who went on to make 81, made many runs for Surrey and England in the 1880s. Once, when demoted to no. 10 by Lord Harris in a Test Match, he responded with 117, still the highest ever Test score from that position. Another very interesting player in the Surrey side was the young William Lockwood. He was only 19 at the time of the game, but he developed into one of the best fast bowlers of his generation. He played in twelve Tests and contributed greatly to Surrey's run of championship wins.

Although Montague's Blackheath playing career was curtailed that year, his work for the club off the field increased. He became Match Manager for five fixtures. The job of a Match Manager was to raise a side appropriate to the opposition and to handle administrative duties such as finding umpires and agreeing start times. It was another responsible role for Montague. He was still on the Committee and remained a cricket director of the club.

In order to strengthen the management of the club still further, three honorary Vice Presidents were appointed. They were Viscount Lewisham MP, Lord Hillingdon and none other than Lord Harris. Montague therefore saw Lord Harris in action as a committee member at first hand and became aware of his firm leadership ethic, with which Kent and the MCC would become familiar. All the indications are that the two got on well on and off the field.

Lord Harris could be a formidable and intemperate man. It was said that Oscar Wilde based the part of Lady Bracknell, the bossy mother in *The Importance of Being Earnest*, on a female version of Lord Harris. Yet for fifty years he was the cornerstone of Kent cricket, and at the MCC he served as a Committee member, Trustee, Treasurer, and President. With the exception of W.G. Grace, he was the most influential figure in the international development of cricket. It was a brave man who argued any point with him. Once in a club match he was offended by one of the opposition bowlers. 'You Sir,' he stormed, 'are a disgrace. Go home.' And the poor man did. The bowler neither received nor expected any support from his own captain. The reason for Harris's displeasure was undoubtedly because he considered the bowler a 'chucker'. A few years earlier Harris had withdrawn from the Gentlemen's side at Lord's as he felt Alfred Evans's bowling action was suspect. This was the same Alfred Evans who had kept Montague out of the Oxford side.

On 3 February 1931 Lord Harris sent out what he imperiously described as a Birthday Message via *The Times*. He was 80 and still in office, but perhaps showing signs of too much time spent fielding in the sun without a cap. In the Message he extolled the merits of cricket. 'You will do well to love it for it is more free from anything sordid, anything dishonourable than any game in the world. To play keenly, honourably, generously and self-sacrificingly is a moral lesson in itself and the classroom is God's air and sunshine.' He died a year later and so was spared having to adjudicate on the Bodyline furore. His successors at Lord's, with their blunt rejection of Australian complaints and support for the intimidatory assault of Jardine's fast bowlers, had not taken the Message to heart.

However, even Lord Harris was not immune from paying deference to the social order. Once he appeared in the royal enclosure at Ascot dressed in a brown suit instead of the regulation top hat and tails. Edward VII was not impressed: 'Oh hello, Harris,' he said, 'been rattin'?'

Lord Harris must have liked and respected the work Montague did for Blackheath and approved of him personally, otherwise Montague would not have got near a Blackheath committee room, never mind become a director of the club. That Montague forged such a relationship with Lord Harris was arguably his greatest achievement.

SEVEN

A Happy Wanderer

Throughout Montague's time at Blackheath, Oxford and earlier at Winchester, he had enjoyed the company of many well-known people, often cricketers. Although Blackheath was now the centre of his cricket, his circle had always been much wider. He played for several teams in the West Country, and he extended his contacts and reputation with 'wandering' cricket. Wandering clubs were clubs with no home ground whose qualification to play depended on the terms set down by the founders. Sometimes the invitation to play was confined to old boys of specific public schools, although often men were asked simply on the basis of being good players and amusing social company.

Four men invented wandering cricket one evening in July 1845. They were Cambridge undergraduates who 'found themselves at supper at the Blenheim Hotel in Bond Street'. Their names were Frederick Ponsonby (later Lord Bessborough), his brother Spencer Ponsonby (later Sir Spencer Ponsonby-Fane), John Baldwin and R.P. Long. W.P. Bolland was appointed Perpetual President and twenty other gentlemen were chosen to make up what was to be known as 'I Zingari'. Appropriately for a wandering side, this translates from the Italian as 'The Gypsies'. The club colours were to be black, red and gold although the origins of the choice are unknown. Perhaps they represent the adage 'out of darkness, through fire, into light'. More improbably, but more romantically, they may represent the orders given by the King of the Hejaz 'out of the land of Egypt, through the Red Sea, into the Promised Land'. The choice of members reflected the preferences of the founders. They were selected, never elected, on the basis of 'good repute and likely to play the game in its true spirit'. This usually meant royalty, aristocracy, senior members of the military and old boys of the top public schools. George V and Edward VIII became members. To this day it remains the most exclusive of the wandering clubs, although for the first century of its existence it was also the most self-important.

In 1859 in a match against Wimbledon played on the Common, I Zingari turned up a man short. When Wimbledon's last man came out to bat, I Zingari refused to continue, on the basis, presumably, that it was ungentlemanly for Wimbledon to take advantage of their extra man. Faced with a cabal of toffs made up of two Lords, three Honourables and a substantial military presence, Wimbledon gracefully conceded to this baseless objection. They then quietly ensured that the incident would be recalled for the next 150 years.

I Zingari were furious when soon after the end of the First World War Germany adopted the same black, red and gold colours for their national flag. It was too much for the membership and the following protest was submitted: 'We the members of I Zingari, desire to lodge emphatic protest against the degradation of our colours.'

TO GERMANY

Your fleet you've scuttled, and your War Lords fled,
Your 'toasted day' has turned to night instead;
Crime upon crime, your last crime now we see
You've 'pinched' the colours of I Zingari.
The colours that we love, Black, Red and Gold,

Round which our splendid story has been told;
'Neath which we've taught you how to 'play the game',
Must ne'er be sullied by your deeds of shame.
Our 'Freemen' will know how to treat the foe,
So Beatty, Haig, and French and Jellicoe
Of this last crime give them the dregs to drink,
And with your 'Freemen' tell them what we think.

Today's satirical scriptwriters would pay well for such a verse. The more historically alert would be outraged at the sentimental commemoration of four men who were the architects of the slaughter of land and sea in 1914–18. The four were all members of I Zingari and indeed were given the Freedom of I Zingari for their wartime services. Even the I Zingari might have hesitated if they had realised that at the Battle of Passchendaele, for example, each inch of land gained cost a British life. In cricketing terms this meant nearly 800 men died to gain the length of a 22-yard pitch. One wonderful player who contributed an inch was Colin Blythe, a spin bowler for Kent and England. He died with the King's Own Light Infantry at Passchendaele in November 1917. This, though, was 1920, and the protest was seen as honourable and justified. It was ignored, and Germany continues to fly I Zingari colours. In fact Germany's use of the colours dates from the early nineteenth century, so if anyone had a basis for complaint it was the Germans against I Zingari.

Some I Zingari members had been upset when, in 1867, the MCC adopted two of their colours, red and gold. The fact that the MCC was formed in the previous century mattered not. The protest, which was also doomed to failure, contrasted with the MCC's more generous spirit when Watford Football Club chose red-and-gold turnovers to their socks. No complaint was made.

Montague never came into contact with I Zingari but his brother Edward was selected a member in 1901, shortly after he had stopped playing for the Royal Engineers. No doubt his military career helped in his selection. Nevertheless this was quite an achievement. Even W.G. Grace had to lean on an I Zingari official to secure the selection of his two sons as his letter dated 20 February 1904 to a Mr Alfred Marsh shows: 'Now I want to know if you have anything to do with regards to the election of members for the I Z cricket club. I want my sons W.G. Junior and H.E. made members if it is possible. As they are both connected with the Navy it would be so nice if they belonged to the I Z. I know you will put in a good word for them.' Selection was not easy. H.E. went on to become a Vice-Admiral, but W.G. Junior died the following year after an appendicitis operation on the Isle of Wight, aged 31.

Edward made his mark against the I Zingari as an 18-year-old playing for the Royal Military Academy. He had a bowling analysis of 7 wickets for 12 runs. These were amazing figures against such good opposition. Edward was an all-rounder and is described in *A History of Royal Engineers Cricket* as 'a dear good fellow and a very reliable bowler. He could bowl all day. He could generally be relied upon to make 20–30 runs in a dignified and sound manner.' Like Montague he thrived on a variety of clubs, and the status of these clubs was even better than Montague's. In addition to I Zingari, he played for the Free Foresters, Oxford Harlequins, Household Brigade and Yorkshire Gentlemen. Apart from the Band of Brothers, it would be hard to improve on this list.

Montague and Edward both played against the Band of Brothers. Montague did so three times, twice for Blackheath and once for West Kent. Edward played twice, both times for the Royal Engineers, but in the first of these he retired hurt and took no further part.

The Band of Brothers was formed in 1858 on the spur of the moment by officers in the East Kent Yeomanry who wished to continue the fun they had had under canvas during Yeomanry training at Dover. It soon became a cricket club, and has remained a highly respected, strong team based on Kent cricket. In August 2003 its junior section, the BaBes, celebrated its centenary under the chairmanship of Lord Kingsdown. The club is of similar status to I Zingari.

Colours and clothes were always important to wandering sides. The most exotic blazer ever designed belonged to the Butterflies

Cricket Club: it was made of plain white silk, and the players' ladies were invited to sew or embroider onto it butterflies of whatever colour, size or design they wished. Montague would not have got to wear this elegant jacket, as the design proved too expensive and lasted only one season. It was replaced by a jacket almost as gaudy in magenta, black and mauve.

The club was formed in 1863 by a group of Rugby schoolboys known as the Pantaloons. It soon became the Butterflies and drew its membership from former pupils of Rugby, Eton, Harrow, Charterhouse, Westminster and Winchester schools. Montague was therefore eligible, and it was precisely the sort of good, exclusive cricket that he would have enjoyed. Unfortunately, records and scorebooks for the club between 1875 and 1914 have nearly all been destroyed, but we know for certain that Montague played at least once. This was on 14 June 1883, when he turned out against the College at Winchester. Also in the Butterflies side that day was Alexander Webbe.

The Butterflies have an illustrious history. In 1865 they were the first club to visit Paris and play the local team at the Pelouse de Madrid in the Bois de Boulogne. The team enjoyed themselves to the extent that 'some of our team saying "goodnight" in too boisterous a manner, were seized by gendarmes and locked up for the night'. They were rescued the next morning by the British Ambassador.

Over the years, thirteen Butterflies have captained England, including the ubiquitous Douglas Jardine. This was the fifth cricket club he had in common with Montague. The club maintains its membership criteria to this day, and far from being an anachronism is as flourishing as ever. Its fixture list includes the Eton Ramblers, Stragglers of Asia and Chelsea Arts Club. In his book *Famous Cricket Clubs*, H.E. Powell-Jones says, 'Their cricket is as gay as their colours.' An ambiguous comment now, but a harmless compliment in 1928.

Montague qualified as a wandering cricketer on two counts. He played for wandering sides, notably the Incogniti, and he himself wandered between many clubs especially in the Bournemouth area. These included the Gentlemen of Dorset, the Gentlemen of

Bournemouth, Canford Manor and the Old Wykehamists. He played for Kingston Park while still at university, and continued to do so for each season until his death. The highlight of his career was playing for Kingston Park against the Ishmaelites during the latter's West Country tour at Dorchester in August 1883. Montague took all 10 wickets in the Ishmaelites' first innings, a marvellous feat at any level of cricket. He played regularly for Dorset in Minor Counties matches against Devon, Wiltshire and Somerset, and invariably took wickets. His best effort, also in 1883, was 12 wickets in a match against Wiltshire at Trowbridge. Montague played a few times for the Old Wykehamists, but the club was almost dormant in 1880–4 when he would have been most active.

Apart from the pleasure of playing cricket in a variety of competitive and enjoyable situations, these matches gave Montague an opportunity to make new friends. Often they were from socially well-connected families. It was in 1883 when he was playing his best wandering cricket that he was nominated to become a member of the MCC.

Montague's most successful cricket with wandering clubs was for the Incogniti. It was, and remains, a club of great traditions. It was formed in 1861, and its mysterious name means 'unknown only to the unknown'. The condition of membership was simple 'good cricket and good fellowship', and this has always been observed. From time to time the club has been graced by some major personalities, in particular Douglas Jardine, who seemed to be following Montague's cricketing footsteps via Winchester and New College. Bernard Bosanquet, inventor of the googly and father of the illustrious newsreader, was a member. His bowling clinched the Ashes at Sydney in 1904. The cricketing talents of Sir Arthur Conan Doyle, the creator of Sherlock Holmes, are less well known, but he turned out for the Incogniti in the early 1900s. He was a good enough player to represent the MCC at Lord's and to dismiss W.G. Grace. It was his only first-class wicket.

The Incogniti tours have always been popular, especially to the West Country, although expeditions to a dozen different countries have also been organised. These include America, Australia and

Holland. It was Montague's fellow housemaster, Frederick Lacey, who first introduced him to the Incogniti. Lacey had been made a member a few years earlier. Montague impressed the Incogniti when he played against them for Blackheath in July 1881 and took 4 wickets. Soon after, playing for Dorset, he made 64 and took 5 wickets, including that of Trevitt Hine-Haycock of Sidmouth and Oxford fame.

These performances won Montague a coveted place on the Incogniti's West Country tour. Apart from the high standard of play, the tour was famous for the 'bread and cheese for lunch, dinner at six and then a great dance with the ladies'. The tour still goes on, but the ladies' night is no more. Montague must have loved the week. He played in four matches, against Bournemouth, Torquay, Exmouth and Sidmouth, and took 25 wickets. He even made 35 against Exmouth. His social life was widening and consolidating. In 1882 Montague played in five matches, including the West Country tour again, and took a creditable 14 wickets. Against the Incogniti for Blackheath in June he took 5 wickets, but from then on Montague's appearances for the Incogniti reduced, and he played only twice in 1884, both times against schools. He missed the fixture against Bexley in June, and so was denied the chance to bowl at a man called Montague Bowden. At 23, Bowden remains the youngest ever England captain. He took over the side in the absence of C. Aubrey Smith for the 2nd Test in South Africa in 1888. He stayed on as a stockbroker, but in 1892 he was travelling with Cecil Rhodes's Pioneer Corps to Rhodesia when he fell from a cart and died. He was buried in a coffin made of whisky cases. Today his signature is the rarest and most costly of all England's Test players.

Montague did not play again for the Incogniti until 1886 and then just once, against Highgate School in July. It was the season when he hardly played any cricket after the end of that month. The next season he played against the Incogniti at the Rectory Field and took 8 wickets over the two innings. It was partly due to this success that he was asked to play two matches with the Incogniti at the end of August on a week-long Welsh tour against Bryn-y-Neuadd. It is the only known time that Montague went outside England. He claimed 13 wickets, so although he was playing fewer matches there was no sign that his skills were in decline.

The visit to play Bryn-y-Neuadd would have been an exciting expedition for Montague. The two matches were played at Llanfairfechan, a seaside resort on the North Wales coast, about 8 miles south-west of Llandudno. Bryn-y-Neuadd or Hall on the Hill was the country-house estate of Sydney Platt. Platt played in both fixtures and had got together a strong scratch side, which included several Incogniti members. He was a wealthy businessman who had made money in the mills of Lancashire, and when he built his imposing home he included a cricket pitch. This was by repute the best pitch in Wales, as Platt decreed it should be based on slate from the nearby Bethesda quarry. Bryn-y-Neuadd often provided country-house cricket for touring sides, particularly from Ireland. The team never played in a league. Although the estate became a private mental hospital in the early 1900s, cricket continued to be played there into the 1950s. Warren Martin, a stalwart of Welsh cricket, recalls playing there against a Bryn-y-Neuadd side that included his father, who was a male nurse at the hospital. Bryn-y-Neuadd's cricket days ended when the whole estate was acquired by the NHS. Today Llanfairfechan is renowned for its pleasant walks, sailing and golf; in Montague's time, before the Menai Bridge was opened, it offered a challenging and dangerous walk across the Straits to Beaumaris.

Perhaps the town's greatest asset in 1887 was its railway station, without which the Incogniti would never have reached the ground, as the railway provided the only practical means of getting the team to its destination. This involved a long journey north to Crewe, and then a change on to the delightful North Wales coastal line, where the railway keeps close to the coast and passes through Rhyl, Abergele, Llandudno and Penmaenmawr before reaching Llanfairfechan. Two other characters from the Ripper 'cast' are remembered in the area. Penmaenmawr was Prime Minister William Gladstone's favourite retreat, and in Llandudno there is a statue of the White Rabbit from *Alice in Wonderland* to mark Charles

Dodgson's frequent visits. The journey through the centre of England and along the top of Wales would have been a whole new world to Montague. For the Incogniti it was an enterprising and ambitious tour, in keeping with the club's traditions before and since.

There is a possibility that Montague did play at Bryn-y-Neuadd two years earlier when a Blackheath side visited there in June 1885. However, detailed records are lost and, as the game was in term time, it may have been difficult for Montague to get so much time off.

The last match Montague played for the Incogniti was on 30 May 1888, against Dulwich College. He took 3 wickets and made 43.

Montague's world of wandering cricket, whether it was with wandering clubs or through his own journeying around a variety of teams, meant he built up a network of contacts. Whomever he met and wherever he played, he always contributed something of interest on or off the field. He was indeed a 'happy wanderer'.

EIGHT

A Magnificent Indulgence

When Montague joined the MCC in 1884 he did so not primarily for social prestige, but to be an active playing member. At the time there were about 3,000 full members, of whom some 250 played in one or more match. The MCC is not a wandering club. It has the finest home ground in the world, and plays a handful of its most senior matches there, but nearly all its fixtures are played away against clubs and schools. These are known as 'out matches'.

MCC records do not exist for 'out matches' for the first two years of Montague's membership, but we do know he played a few times. Montague's first recorded match was on 10 June 1886, when he played for MCC against Harrow School. Also in the MCC side that day was William Attewell, who played in ten Tests between 1884 and 1892, and so was a current England player. He was an excellent medium-paced bowler, so unfortunately Montague's chances to shine were limited. In the same year and the following year Montague turned out against the Clergy of England at Blackheath. In the Clergy side of 1887 was Montague's seconder for MCC membership, the Revd Vernon Royle, who by now had given up his schoolmaster duties for Holy Orders. In the same season, this time playing against the MCC for Blackheath, Montague came up against another player of real class, Arthur Pougher. In 1896 his prodigious spell of bowling helped MCC dismiss the Australians for 18, their lowest ever score. He played for England and had a first-class century to his credit. This time Montague bowled him for 28, en route to taking 4 wickets. When Montague batted, it took the Test-player combination of c. Pougher b. Fothergill to remove him. Arnold Fothergill was yet another cricketer who played for England whom Montague confronted in his career. Montague seemed to do better against the MCC than for them: the previous year in the same fixture he had taken 5 wickets.

Meanwhile Montague's brother Edward had had his application for MCC membership accepted, and he played in at least one match, against Mote Park in August 1887. He took a wicket and made a few runs.

Francis Lacey was one of the most celebrated MCC Secretaries. He went to Trinity College, Cambridge, later qualified as a barrister, and was then, in 1898, appointed to the post, which he held until 1926. He was somewhat dour, but most efficient, and a handsome oil painting of him in morning dress still hangs in the Lord's pavilion. He won a Blue at Cambridge, but his main playing claim to fame was a score of 323 not out in a Minor Counties match for Hampshire, which is still a record. It was in a game between the Incogniti and Bournemouth in August 1881 that Montague and Francis Lacey first met. Montague was playing for the Incogniti and Lacey for Bournemouth, and Montague had a splendid match, taking 12 wickets (although not Lacey's). A year later, this time for Kingston Park against the Incogniti, the two shared a 50-run partnership. Lacey's home was in Wareham, very near Wimborne, and it is quite likely that their families were friends.

Reliable and hardworking as Lacey certainly was as Secretary of the MCC, it has always puzzled pundits why he was the first person chosen to receive a knighthood for services to cricket. W.G. Grace retired from the first-class game in 1899, and his promotion would have been a natural and popular move in the new century's Honours List. Conspiracy theories still rumble around. The reason could have been his financial opportunism – Grace was described in *Wisden* 'as quite breathtakingly grasping when his eye caught the glint of hard cash'. It is estimated that his fees and demands netted him over £1 million by today's values. This greed and a hypocritical stand against professionalism may have been noticed by the authorities and earned him disqualification from higher honours. The journalist Alasdair Reid rates him third in the all-time list of recipients of sporting 'brown envelopes'. Perhaps he had too publicly disapproved of the Prince of Wales' (later Edward VII) dalliances, or perhaps Queen Victoria saw him as a threat to her omnipotence. If there was a reason, it must have been a strong one. Grace was the epitome of the Victorian age and even formed a 'Sporting League' to support the rebuilding of the Empire, Leicester Square. This was a marvellous emporium with a cheerful decadence and had long been a haunt of royalty. It proudly displayed a statue of George I. The young Winston Churchill was an enthusiastic patron. The truth may be more prosaic. The authorities of the early twentieth century rated off-field services more highly than those on-field. Not until 1949 did Sir Donald Bradman change this attitude.

Montague was eligible for probably the grandest and most self-indulgent banquet in the history of cricket. It was to celebrate the Centenary of the MCC, and no expense or effort was spared to ensure it was done properly.

It was held on 15 June 1887, and the venue was Lord's. The precise site was the Tennis Court, which soon afterwards was replaced by the Mound Stand. With so many members and a capacity for only 250 guests, there were strict rules for attendance. For a start members could not apply for tickets – it was by invitation only, and for this the qualification was confusing. All past presidents of the club, and a 'few distinguished supporters of the noble game' were invited. This second group could, of course, include anybody who the committee felt like inviting, and some of the guests would certainly not even have been members. The third group was members 'who had played in the match Gentlemen v Players at Lord's, twice'.

This sounds clear, yet it is a good example of Victorian double standards. Because Players were by definition professionals, none was invited. Of the Lord's side of 1884, all seven amateurs (Gentlemen) were there. The other four were excluded. This meant no place for George Ulyett or Richard Barlow, who both turned out for the Players nine times, nor Arthur Shrewsbury (eight), nor Edmund Peate (four). About twenty Players had appeared in the fixture the qualifying twice. However, despite the massive contribution cricketers like these had made to the English game, they were not considered suitable. Montague as an amateur would have taken precedence.

Amateurs, it seems, were not only entitled to the finer things of life, but owing in part to a combination of diet, medical treatment and lifestyle, they actually lived longer too. Of the same Lord's side the amateurs had a life expectancy of sixty-three years, while the professionals were, on average, dead by the age of 51.

There were forty places at the top table. All but four were taken by those with titles, and these included eighteen Lords. The Chancellor of the Exchequer, the Honourable George Goschen MP, was seated next to the French Ambassador, whose name was William Henri Waddington. He was born in France of a French mother and English father, and was educated at Cambridge, where he had been a friend of Lord Bessborough and his co-founder colleagues of I Zingari. This, together with his English roots, may explain his presence. It might also have been MCC's way of repaying the great hospitality which the club had received about twenty years earlier when the MCC and I Zingari had taken sides to play teams in Paris. This was the first overseas match ever played by MCC. The surviving founders of I Zingari, John Baldwin and Spencer Ponsonby-Fane, were also at the dinner.

The top table was not without a modicum of scandal. Sitting next to John Baldwin was Lord Londesborough. He had been named as one of the co-respondents, along with the Prince of Wales, in the Lillie Langtry divorce petition – a petition that Edward Langtry withdrew when he was offered a diplomatic post abroad.

The assembly was a tour de force of the English establishment, and a wonderful opportunity for the aristocracy to flex its muscles to the exclusion of other ranks, although if Montague had been there he would have seen some familiar faces. His club colleagues Lord Harris and Stanley Christopherson were present, so too were the Hine-Haycocks, father and son. His MCC sponsor, Vernon Royle, was included, as were Alexander Webbe, John Shuter and Alfred Evans. Even the brother of Montague's old headmaster at Winchester, the Revd Charles Ridding, secured a place, and Montague could have asked C.W. Alcock about the description in the *Lillywhite's Annual* that his batting was 'peculiar'. At Winchester Montague had played some football, so he would have been interested to talk to Alcock, not just about the *Lillywhite's Annuals* but because Alcock was the current secretary of the Football Association – a post he held for thirty years. He introduced the FA Cup and is still widely regarded as the creator of international football. If Montague was still short of company there was Kynaston Studd's elder brother, and Ivo Bligh's father, the 7th Lord Darnley. Lastly, if Montague was feeling brave, he could have engaged the guest of honour, George Goschen. Sir George and his younger brother, William, both went to Rugby, and hence were eligible for the Butterflies. William certainly played for them. He later became the British Ambassador in Berlin during the period leading up to the First World War, an especially awkward assignment, as his father was German.

It was not just a gathering of the great and the good of English cricket; it was the opportunity for a statement of upper-class superiority. There were fifteen speeches. Individually and collectively they were a masterly amalgam of pomposity and obsequiousness. The President Chandos Leigh proposed the health of the Queen, and reminded guests they were also celebrating the fiftieth anniversary of 'Her Most Gracious Majesty's reign' and invited guests 'with double zest to drink with loyal lips and loving homage'. He also paid fulsome tribute to the Prince of Wales, and reminded the assembled company that his two sons, Prince Albert Victor (later the ill-fated Duke of Clarence) and Prince George, were

MCC members. In view of Prince Albert Victor's growing and public reputation for dissolute behaviour, this may have unnerved a few people. His reputation was such that even the royal peacocks were not considered safe in his presence.

Representatives of the Lords and the Commons exchanged pleasantries full of analogies between cricket and life. The French Ambassador admitted his knowledge of cricket was 'so small' and then attributed the English qualities 'steadfast, daring, enduring' to the game. He credited cricket with helping to establish the Empire with that 'honest dealing and straight play which had founded everywhere that plucky race of pioneers of discovery'. Sir Saul Samuel replying for the Colonies said that 'All Australians regard themselves as Englishmen.' Today he would be fired or suffocated before the cheese. W.G. Grace spoke for the medical profession, and Lord Harris, never one to be left out, thanked the MCC for allowing the counties to be represented, and ended by proposing the health of the Press, despite 'having considerable differences with the Press on cricket matters'. No one replied for the Press, probably because they were not invited. Even if they had been, by now they would have been asleep, drugged by boredom and champagne.

However, the menu was a credit to the occasion. It was made up of five extensive courses and the highlights were the thick turtle soup, larded sweetbreads on spinach, quarters of lamb, lobster salad, cheese cakes and frozen MCC cricket balls – the last an imaginative pudding made using the most up-to-date technology. There was no recognition on the menu for an earlier French Ambassador to London in the 1820s, Vicomte de Chateaubriand. Nor was the spelling of Lafite, as in Château, perfect. However, the writer of the menu did pay correct tribute to another cut of beef, describing it as Sir Loins. This accolade dated back to 1617 when James I dined at Houghton Tower, and was so taken with the loin of beef that he knighted it saying, 'Arise Sir Loin'. No doubt he had been enjoying the royal wine stocks.

As was the Victorian custom, wines hardly featured at this dinner. Instead there was a choice of six champagnes, and this reflected the fashion at major banquets of the time of drinking champagne throughout the meal. The name of one of these champagnes gave a hint of some under-cover entrepreneurship by the organisers. It was the Leatham and Cator's Crème d'Or 1880. Among the guests were a G.A.B. Leatham and E. Cator. Unusually, the drinks were not supplied by Berry Bros and Rudd, who were the leading wine merchant to the establishment, royalty and aristocracy and whose customer list included Napoleon III, Arthur Balfour, John Nash, Beau Brummell and Lord Byron. (The latter lived conveniently close at Albany, and had champagne sent over to welcome his lover, Lady Caroline Lamb, who was smuggled in disguised as a page boy.) Gerald Leatham was an MCC member and a fair player, but Cator had no first-class record. The suspicion is that Messrs Leatham and Cator negotiated two places at the dinner in return for generous supplies of champagne. Their company no longer exists, and its address, 40 Albemarle Street, is now a fast food café. Berry Bros and Rudd are still thriving on the same site as they did three hundred years ago.

This, then, was the MCC Centenary Dinner and it was magnificent – a piece of social history and a microcosm of the Imperial Victorian age. Montague would not have been the least offended at not being invited. He knew his place in this particular batting order was far from high enough. It is to his credit that, if he had been there, he would not have been out of his depth.

NINE

Liaisons Dangereuses

The seeds of Montague's downfall may have been sown in 1820 with the creation of the Cambridge Conversazione Society. At first it was an innocent debating society set up by undergraduates to discuss literary and religious matters and it soon took on the nickname 'The Apostles', since there were twelve founder members. There had always been an undercurrent of homosexuality in the Apostles, but towards the end of the nineteenth century it was rife and was a considerable help in obtaining election to the society. The Apostles also attracted some of the brightest minds at Cambridge, particularly those at Trinity College.

Montague became involved at the edges of this world when he took up his chambers at 9 King's Bench Walk after his acceptance into the Inner Temple as a barrister in 1885. On the face of it, this was a great achievement and a huge opportunity to fulfil a highly paid and respected professional life. In reality, there were dangers. Montague, for all his intelligence and affability, had really experienced only the narrow confines of school, university and teaching. He may have been eager and naive. Many of the Apostles at that time tended to be in love with themselves and each other and were keen to boost each other's ego with literary and philosophical cleverness. The society also had a harder edge. It had become, partly because of the illegality of homosexuality, secretive and self-protective. Many of its members were from professional backgrounds such as the Law, and had had a wider range of experiences than Montague.

This mixture of intellect, experience and status appealed to Montague, who found it bold and attractive. It was not long before he met Henry Stephen, who resided 50 yards away at 3 King's Bench Walk, and Henry's brother, Herbert, who had chambers opposite. Even closer, on the floor below Montague, was his old Fives opponent from Oxford, Reginald Dyke Acland, whose brother, Theodore, was married to Caroline, the daughter of Sir William Gull. Sir William was doctor to Queen Victoria and the Stephen brothers. Edward Henslowe Bedford, the solicitor who, in 1889, helped cover up the Cleveland Street scandal, also lived at No. 9. The Inns of Court was a close-knit, influential place.

Another Stephen brother, James, had chambers nearby in Lincoln's Inn, and his closest friend was Harry Wilson. Like James Stephen, Wilson was an Apostle, and he too proved to be a considerable sexual roué. Wilson's house by the Thames at Chiswick, called The Osiers, was known as a 'chummery' where homosexuals were welcome to drop in for an evening or a night. Naturally, only gentlemen of sufficient social standing would be admitted.

The Duke of Clarence was the eldest son of the Prince of Wales and therefore in direct line to the throne. He was a longstanding friend of Harry Wilson and James Stephen and knew about The Osiers. The following letters from the Duke to Wilson underline this friendship. In February 1888 the Duke wrote:

Dear Harry,
    I was very glad to hear from you again and it is good of you to think of asking me to come to your place to see the boat race from. I should be delighted to do so for it would be very nice to

meet some of our old Cambridge friends again whom I have not seen for some time. But the question is whether I shall be in town then or not at the end of March for if I am not I fear I shall be detained at York then by my duties with my regiment. But I had better let you know again for certain a little later on if that would be the same to you.

A few weeks later the Duke wrote in a follow-up letter: 'I now find very much to my regret that I shall not be able to get away next Saturday which is very tiresome for I should much have enjoyed paying you a visit at Chiswick and seeing some of my old friends again.'

Today, The Osiers is still an impressive house, with a lovely garden leading down to the Thames at Chiswick Mall. It would have been an ideal retreat, so little wonder that the Duke regretted being unable to join the party.

Trinity College library at Cambridge holds the diary of Harry Wilson written between 1883 and 1887, and in it Wilson mentions John Henry Lonsdale. Lonsdale's address in the diary is 5 Eliot Cottages, Blackheath, a stone's throw from Montague's school. Furthermore, Lonsdale was a barrister, and his accommodation was at 4 King's Bench Walk. This was next door to Henry Stephen and a few yards away from Montague. It is inconceivable that all three men did not know each other. If further confirmation were needed, it came in 1887, when Lonsdale gave up the Law for the Church. His first ministry was at Wimborne Minster. Perhaps Montague was able to use his influence to help Lonsdale into such a prestigious first appointment.

As if to avoid any doubt about his sexual preferences, Wilson wrote in another diary entry against the name of Henry Stephen: 'I love him, I love him.' He also noted: 'Nov 2 dine with hrh, jek studd, hc goodhart, ronald etc to cust's later.' 'Hrh' was the Duke of Clarence and the others are easily identifiable – J.E.K. Studd, H.C. Goodhart, Lord Ronald Sutherland Gower and Harry Cust. All were well-known homosexuals. The occasion gives an insight into the Duke's choice of dining companions. The diary also records sundry invitations to Sandringham and to the Duke's private rooms. After this unconventional and risky early life, Wilson developed into something of an establishment figure. He held various posts in the colonial service, became chairman of British Overseas Stores Ltd and was knighted in 1919 by George V, the younger brother of the Duke of Clarence. His credentials, once the Duke had moved on, were immaculate. He died aged 78.

Through the Stephen brothers, Montague met their sibling, James. James Kenneth Stephen was seen as brilliant, witty and eccentric and had been a member of the Apostles since 1879. In 1883 he was appointed tutor to the Duke of Clarence. Stephen's task was to prepare the Duke for entrance to Trinity College, Cambridge – a labour that even Hercules might have found challenging.

James Stephen, or 'Jem' to his friends, was the son of the High Court judge Sir James Fitzjames Stephen. Both were Apostles. He was also a cousin of Virginia Woolf, the novelist, and she, as a 4-year-old, found him frightening. She was nervous of his deep voice and intense blue eyes and she found his behaviour erratic and slightly mad. Once he burst into her nursery brandishing a sword. Stephen may have been bi-sexual, as he made prolonged and unwelcome advances to Stella Duckworth, Virginia Woolf's elder half-sister. His uncontrolled manner was accentuated by a head injury, which he sustained during a New Year visit to Felixstowe in 1886 when staying with his friends the Cobbolds at The Lodge. They were a wealthy banking and brewing family. Stephen was out riding along a coastal bridal path, and after a while reached Walton Mill. He was looking at the steam engine that worked the mill when a whistle from an approaching dock train frightened his horse. It reared up and Stephen was thrown. The doctor who attended him later in London was Sir William Gull.

It seems that Felixstowe was a popular watering hole for wealthy families at this time. Arthur Balfour was captain of Felixstowe Ferry Golf Club in 1889. He, like his two sons Francis and Gerald, was an Apostle. His commitment to the club and to golf in general was summarised when he explained his personal philosophy: 'Give me my tools, my golf clubs and leisure, and I would ask for nothing more. My ideal in life is to read a lot, write a little, play plenty of golf and have nothing to worry about.' Somewhere along the line over the next thirteen years this idyllic life plan fell apart. In 1902 he became Prime Minister.

Edward Fitzgerald, the poet, described the Deben, which enters the North Sea at Felixstowe, as 'the Queen of rivers', and it was on this river that he would sail his yacht named *Scandal*. Eventually he sold the boat, a two-ton schooner, to a Cuthbert Quilter, a local Felixstowe businessman, benefactor and MP, for £200. Quilter renamed the yacht *Sapphire*. Fitzgerald once rented a house in Felixstowe for three months on doctor's orders but spent most of his time sailing at Woodbridge or in Norfolk visiting a particularly hefty fisherman. The Prince of Wales brought his son, George, occasionally, and in 1891 the German Empress arrived with an enormous entourage. James Stephen's choice of Felixstowe as a holiday resort was therefore normal. It is possible he played a round of golf with Arthur Balfour and visited the Dyke Aclands at their large holiday home called Dunkery.

At this time Virginia Woolf was too young to understand the Ripper story, but with two close relatives involved (and, in the case of James Stephen, a suspect), she would have heard it discussed in later years as part of the family folklore. The extent to which she absorbed it in detail became tragically clear many years after. Several members of the Apostles became an integral part of her life. She knew Roger Fry, the art critic, for many years and wrote his biography, omitting the matter of his affair with her sister Vanessa. Leonard Woolf, whom she married, was so thrilled to be elected to the Apostles brotherhood that his Cambridge studies suffered. Woolf and her friends and contemporaries went on to be central to the influential Bloomsbury set. But she did not have an unreserved admiration of the Apostles: her view of them was more thoughtful and accurate than most. She believed 'they were clever and unworldly but arrogant, prickly and withdrawn. They were men who tended to be devoid of female company.'

A fine portrait of James Stephen hangs in King's College Cambridge. It was painted in 1887 by Charles Wellington Furse, and this work may have been his introduction to the Stephen family. It was through Stephen's cousin Virginia that Furse met and married Katherine, a childhood friend of Virginia. Furse died of tuberculosis, aged 36, so a career as a 'bold voluptuous painter' was never properly fulfilled.

Like Montague, James Stephen qualified as a barrister, but never received a brief. However, it is unlikely that he resorted to special pleading legal work, as he had access to ample funds from his father. In 1889 Sir James presided over the trial of Florence Maybrick, who was accused of poisoning her husband, James. James Maybrick was subsequently identified as a strong Ripper suspect when some papers, allegedly written by him, came to light years later. The manner in which James Stephen's father handled the Maybrick trial attracted much criticism as he seemed to steer the jury into a guilty verdict. The death sentence was soon commuted to life imprisonment by the Home Secretary, Henry Matthews, and Florence Maybrick was eventually released in 1904. It was another strange link between Montague and the murders through his Apostle connections.

Montague's associations with friends of the Duke of Clarence went back to his schooldays. In the Eton side that Montague played against in 1876 were Evelyn Ruggles-Brise, who became Personal Private Secretary to Home Secretary Henry Matthews, Kynaston Studd and Henry Goodhart. The latter was an Apostle and confidant of the Duke. It was Ruggles-Brise who, in 1896, as Chairman of the Prison Commission, allowed a friend of Oscar Wilde called Frank Harris to visit him in Reading prison to check on Wilde's health. Wilde had been imprisoned the year before following the notorious trial concerning his relationship with Lord Alfred Douglas. Prison conditions were very bad prior to the Prison Act in 1898, and Ruggles-Brise was advised that Wilde might not survive. As a result of Ruggles-Brise's intervention, conditions for Wilde were eased, and he was allowed books and writing materials. Ruggles-Brise became one of the leading British penal reformers of the early twentieth century, and was knighted in 1902.

Montague had other links to the contemporary movers and shakers. Another tutor and guardian to the Duke, Canon John

Neale Dalton, was educated at Blackheath Proprietary School. This school sent many pupils to Trinity College, Cambridge. Dalton and his brother Cornelius were pupils at the Proprietary at the same time as George Valentine's brother, William – the same William who was a team-mate and fellow committee member at Blackheath for several years with Montague. For a short time Cornelius had chambers in the Inner Temple close to Montague's. The chances are that Montague and Cornelius Dalton had several mutual friends and therefore Montague had another possible connection to the royal family.

Dalton owed his position as tutor to the Duke of Clarence (or Prince Albert Victor, as he then was) to the patronage of Queen Victoria, whose approval he had gained as a young clergyman at Whippingham, on the Isle of Wight. She liked his disciplined autocratic style, and her support may have given Dalton the courage to advise the Prince of Wales that the 'abnormally dormant condition of his [son's] mental powers' might be stimulated by a world tour. This duly happened, and in 1879 Albert Victor and his younger brother George set out for a series of cruises on HMS *Bacchante*. The tour lasted nearly three years, and at the end of it the two princes, having received instruction from Dalton, were confirmed by Archbishop Tate at Whippingham in the presence of Queen Victoria.

Dalton had accompanied the ship as the Royal Naval Chaplain and royal guardian, but Victoria's choice may not have been entirely fortunate. At Cambridge Dalton had been the closest friend of Edward Carpenter, a lifelong homosexual. Their relationship has been described as one of the 'greatest intimacy, affection and concern'. Dalton's firm views did produce the occasional eccentricity. Once, to illustrate a scholarly lecture, he insisted on the exhumation of the corpse of Henry VI. He also adopted a young man called Patrick McGill as his protégé. Invariably described as a confirmed bachelor, Dalton suddenly married in middle age. The bride was Catherine Alicia Evan-Thomas, although it was believed that he was keener on her brother Hugh, who had served as midshipman on HMS *Bacchante*. Hugh Evan-Thomas was unaffected by this attention. He became a distinguished First World War admiral and collected notable honours, including a knighthood. A son was born to Dalton and Catherine, named, predictably, Edward.

The best man at their wedding was diarist A.C. Benson, who was referred to as the 'object of [Dalton's] adoration' during his Cambridge days. Benson was not an Apostle, but he had most of the credentials. He spoke in favour of 'romantic friendship within exclusively male communities' and 'the normality of both men and women forming highly emotional relationships with those of their own sex'. He also professed a love for William Johnson, an Eton schoolmaster and another Apostle. Today Benson is remembered as the author of the Empire hymn 'Land of Hope and Glory'. So, for the Duke of Clarence, with Dalton and James Stephen as tutors and their friends as role models, the formative influences are obvious. The clique was cosy, and Montague was a part of it.

The best evidence that Montague had met, and was on friendly terms with, the Duke of Clarence came when Lord and Lady Wimborne invited Montague to Canford on 17 December 1888 for a Grand Ball and Shooting Party in honour of the Duke. The invitation was also to his mother and his sister Georgiana, but not the eldest son, and now head of the family, William. The Victorians were very aware of etiquette, and William's exclusion looked like a snub. It is likely that the Wimbornes knew of the Duke's friendship with Montague and wished to provide some welcoming faces for His Highness. Unfortunately, by the time the event took place Montague was dead, his mother was in an asylum in Brighton and Georgiana was living in New Cross, pregnant with the second of her four children. The invitations were sent out at short notice, probably early December, but it does seem that the Wimbornes were by then not very up to date with the movements of the Druitt family.

A further connection between Montague and the Duke was that Montague's younger brother Edward had been in the same regiment as the artist Frank Miles, and Miles's brother, Major Miles, had been the Duke's army instructor at Aldershot. The Major did pass the comment that he was 'quite astounded at his ignorance'.

Frank Miles was a middle-ranking Victorian artist who specialised in marine and portrait work. The Prince of Wales commissioned him to draw both his wife, Princess Alexandra, and his mistress, Lillie Langtry. Miles's work on Langtry earned him more money than anything else he did. He was also one of Oscar Wilde's lovers. When Wilde came down from Oxford in summer 1879, he and Miles shared rooms at 13 Salisbury Street, off The Strand, where they entertained actresses and beauties. Miles drew the pictures, Wilde wrote the sonnets. About a year later they moved to separate addresses in Tite Street, Chelsea. Next door to Miles at No. 28 lived the American water-colourist James Whistler. Walter Sickert, one of his pupils, often visited him there. Across the road at 9 Tite Street was Sir Melville Macnaghten, soon to be Chief Constable of the Metropolitan Police, who would eventually name Montague as the murderer. The Prince of Wales was a frequent visitor to Wilde's house, and dinner parties would involve all those individuals, including, in all probability, Macnaghten. Miles died in 1891 aged 39, at Brislington Lunatic Asylum, near Bristol. He had been destroyed by his father's insistence that he must give up his relationship with Wilde.

Montague and Wilde were contemporaries at Oxford, but if they did ever meet it is unlikely that the two would have got on very well. Wilde had no interest in cricket or the Law, and he once remarked: 'Being dead is the most boring experience in life, that is if one excepts being married, or dining with a school master.'

There is no doubt that Montague became a member of this barristers' inner circle and dined regularly at the Inns of Court with his group of new friends although his skill at cricket would not have impressed his Apostle colleagues. Of the 250 or so members listed up to 1914, only one, the Hon. Alfred Lyttleton, had real success on the cricket field. This was the same man who kept wicket to Stanley Christopherson in the Lord's Test of 1884. Described as 'tall, handsome and affable', he became an MP and was President of the MCC. He too was a barrister and a good friend of Prime Minister William Gladstone. He went to Trinity College, Cambridge, as did his brother Charles, who was also an Apostle. Alfred died when he was hit on the head by a cricket ball in a club match.

At the MCC Centenary Dinner, attended by 250 of the most influential and best-educated men in the country, Alfred Lyttleton was the only Apostle. The only other guest at the dinner who would have been much interested in the Apostles' creed was the Chancellor Sir George Goschen. At Oxford he had belonged to the Mutual Improvement Society, which modelled itself on the Cambridge Apostles. It was one of the university clubs set up in the 1840s as a serious discussion society rather than as an excuse for eating and drinking. The Mutual believed 'it served to clear up members' views on important subjects'. Eating and drinking proved more popular and in twenty years it was gone. Nor was another of Montague's cricket associates and graduate of Trinity College, Francis Lacey, an Apostle.

Probably Montague's best cricket-related card that he had to play was his friendship with Lord Wimborne, at whose Canford Manor cricket ground he had been a welcome guest for many years. This would have meant something to Harry Wilson and his colleagues, as Lord Wimborne often socialised with the Duke of Clarence. James Stephen was not a cricketer, but he did have some sporting talent. In 1877 he captained the Collegers Eleven in the Eton Wall Game, and the previous year played in the side with his lifelong friend Henry Goodhart. In 1875 another familiar persona, Evelyn Ruggles-Brise, played for the Oppidans. This was a unique achievement in the history of the Wall Game, as for the two previous years he had played for the Oppidans, and no one had represented both sides before.

It would be wrong to believe that every person who went to Trinity College during this period had ambitions to be an Apostle. It was only a small minority who had any interest in joining the club, and the reputation of Trinity was not affected for better or worse. The College's distinction was uninterrupted. Jeremy Paxman points out in his book *The English* that Trinity has produced more Nobel prize winners than the whole of France. The lack of common ground between the Apostles and the cricket fraternity is borne out by the members of a cricket side formed by Trinity College called the Iceni. Of the twenty-one players listed in the mid-1870s, none was an Apostle. Unlike the Snarks at New College, Oxford, the Iceni was not simply a social side. William Patterson, their captain, made a century in the university match in 1876. Philip Morton, too, was almost as talented.

The name Iceni may have been an oblique reference to the unpopularity of Catholicism at the time. The original Iceni were a British tribe led in AD 60 by Boadicea, the wife of King Prasutagus. She was described by a Roman writer as 'in appearance most terrifying, her eye most fierce, and her voice harsh'. On her father's death, the Queen led an uprising in East Anglia against the occupying Romans to rid the country of the invaders and all their influences. For a short time the Iceni were successful, and according to Tacitus killed up to 70,000 Romans and captured London. Soon, however, they themselves were slaughtered and Boadicea poisoned. The cricket team did not last long either.

So strong did the association between James Stephen and Montague become, and such were the royal connections of the former, that one theory suggested that the two committed the Ripper murders together to protect the Duke of Clarence from scandal. This at least supports the view that James Stephen and Montague were close friends. The world of debating, dining and social aggrandisement had always been attractive to Montague; now to this were added elements of the artistic and eccentric, and they must have proved irresistible.

The Apostles continue to this day. A list of the better known includes Alfred Tennyson, Edward Marsh, William Harcourt, Peter Shore and Bertrand Russell. Alfred Tennyson, an early member, embraced the philosophies of the Apostles as eagerly as he did another member, Arthur Hallam. Hallam died aged 22 of a brain haemorrhage in Vienna. It was to commemorate him that Tennyson wrote the long elegiac poem 'In Memoriam'. Tennyson married Emily Sellwood in 1850, and when she gave birth to a son, he insisted he be called Hallam. 'I cannot resist my desire to add the name of my old friend Hallam.' Lady Tennyson wanted the child to be named Alfred, but she was overruled. She said wistfully: 'They will not let me call him Alfred.'

The poet must have had a cricket gene somewhere in his body, as his grandson, also bearing the Hallam name, played nine Tests for England. He inherited some of his grandfather's flamboyance. His cricket was described as bucolic, and when captain of Hampshire he employed the wicket keeper as his butler.

Alfred Tennyson is still celebrated as Trinity College's favourite son, and his statue stands in the College Chapel.

In 1892 Bertrand Russell the philosopher was elected to the Apostles. Russell was held in huge esteem by many of the country's intelligentsia. Yet he was memorably described by a Christ's Hospital schoolboy, Michael Skinner, as a 'moth eaten old windbag'. This dismayed a fellow classmate, Alan Ryan, who went on to be Professor of Politics at Oxford University, the author of a book about Russell, and Warden of Montague's old Oxford college. Skinner became an international lawyer.

It was always likely that, with several Apostles and their friends as such close neighbours in chambers, Montague would be drawn into some of their extraneous activities. This may have gone no further than philosophical and political discussion or poetry reading, but the temptation was there to explore their world more thoroughly. There was the added prospect of meeting senior political and aristocratic figures and possibly even royalty, and it would have been surprising if Montague had been so focused on his work as a prospective barrister that he rejected these other avenues without examination. He may not have appreciated that even by dabbling in them he was entering a powerful, secretive and ultimately dangerous league. It was far removed from the gentlemanly world of cricket.

Montague was born on 15 August, which made his star sign Leo. The astrologer Shelley von Strunckel writing in the London *Evening Standard* may have been uncannily accurate in a recent assessment of Leos. 'You always explore intriguing ideas, people and places, but that doesn't mean that you want to include them in your life.' Even if Montague 'smoked but did not inhale', he was at risk.

TEN

Last of the Summer Wine

The summer of 1888 was variable for the wine fields of France. The burgundy was rated 'excellent', but the chablis 'disappointing'. Montague's year was similarly unsettled. Enjoyable cricket was offset by concerns about his mother. New Year celebrations in the Druitt family would have been muted. Their father had been dead for two years, and the health of their mother was declining. Her illusions, irrational fears and erratic behaviour were becoming worse, and the family was no longer the tight-knit unit of a few years before. The eldest daughter Georgiana was by now married to William Hough, who taught mathematics at Wimborne Grammar School, and their first child, Margaret, had been born six months earlier in June. Also that year Hough had decided to enter the Church and had transferred to the Corpus Christi College Mission in Camberwell, so the family had moved to Forest Hill in south-east London. This was in the vicinity of Blackheath. In the autumn the family moved to New Cross, which was even closer to Montague's school. Edward had long since finished at the Royal Military Academy, and now was an officer in the Royal Engineers based at Chatham. It was as if the Druitts were gravitating towards south-east London.

William, the eldest son, was the head of the family in the absence of his father and during the illness of his mother. He had a burgeoning career as a solicitor in Wimborne and was unmarried. He would remain so for the rest of his life. The movements of Arthur, the youngest son, are unknown, although by now he would have finished university, and probably was back living at Westfield House. Edith, the second daughter, was 20 and would not yet have left Wimborne, and Ethel was only 16. Even if the children all made an effort and assembled at Westfield House, the days of happy family Christmases were over. It is possible to imagine any reunion as being somewhat forced and owing more to obligation than to eager anticipation. Quite possibly, Georgiana and her new baby stayed in Forest Hill, and entertained Edward, who was stationed nearby. As for Montague, the school would be closed, and 9 King's Bench Walk unsuitable for the holiday period, so the likelihood is he returned to Wimborne.

The New Year and new term began routinely for Montague. He was now in his eighth year at the school, and he knew the procedures and curriculum inside out. It was a rather dull way to earn essential money. To offset this boredom, during a long tedious night duty, Montague could have mused on the fine cricketers he had played with or against since his days at Winchester. He would have been able to pick an imaginary team, led by himself, that would have held its own against any opposition. It could have been composed as follows, in batting order:

1. John Shuter (Surrey and England). Fourteen seasons captain of Surrey; 8 first-class hundreds.
2. Robert Abel (Surrey and England). Exceeded 1,000 runs in a season 14 times; 12 first-class hundreds in 1900; 132 not out vs Australians at Sydney.
3. Walter Read (Surrey and England). His 117 still remains highest for a no. 10 in Test cricket; twice captained England; exceeded 1,000 runs in a season 9 times.

4. Francis Lacey (Cambridge and Hampshire). Cricket's first Knight; 323 not out for Hampshire – still a Minor Counties record; MCC Secretary 1898–1926.
5. The Hon. Ivo Bligh (8th Earl of Darnley) (England, Kent, Cambridge). 4 Blues; captain of England team that regained Ashes in 1883; President of MCC.
6. 4th Lord Harris (England, Kent, Oxford). 3 Blues; captain of England; Captain, Secretary and President of Kent; every committee position, including President for MCC.
7. Arthur Pougher (Leicestershire and England). Spin bowler; took 5 wickets for 0 runs vs Australians 1896; scored 1,000 runs and took 100 wickets in one season.
8. William Lockwood (Surrey and England). Fast bowler; 12 Tests; took 100 wickets in a season 7 times and made 15 first-class centuries.
9. Alfred Shaw (Nottinghamshire and England). Medium/slow bowler; 100 wickets in a season 9 times; bowled the first ball in Test cricket.
10. Stanley Christopherson (Kent and England). Fast bowler; took 7 wickets for Gentlemen vs Players in 1884 and in the same year 11 wickets in match vs Australians; record tenure as President of MCC 1939–45.

Montague modestly but correctly would have put himself in last. The side would have been formidably strong, especially in batting, but its obvious flaw was that it lacked a wicketkeeper. To solve this problem Montague could have allowed himself one guest player, in which case he would have included the Hon. Alfred Lyttleton. Francis Lacey would have had to make way. Lyttleton was a contemporary of all the members of the side, a magnificent wicketkeeper and very good batsman. His pedigree was classic Victorian aristocracy. In addition he captained Eton, won four Blues for Cambridge and four caps for England. He also represented the Old Etonians in the 1876 FA Cup Final and played football for England. He was, of course, an Apostle. In short, he had class, style, brains, and talent in abundance.

Montague would have chosen as twelfth man his old friend from Oxford Herbert Webbe.

If Montague needed replacements or favoured the squad system, there were always Alec and George Hearne, Kynaston Studd, Trevitt Hine-Haycock, Vernon Royle, William Attewell, William Patterson and Alfred Evans to step in. Montague clearly was never of the same ability as his team-mates, but at club level his own performances were good. If the squad is taken as a whole, Montague had personally dismissed most of them. Even in this company he could hold his own.

The real cricket season for Montague started promptly on 5 May with a match against the Royal Naval College at the Rectory Field. Two weeks later he had one of his best days, taking 6 wickets for 66 runs against the Royal Artillery. The following Whit Monday and Tuesday he played for Blackheath against one of his other clubs, the Incogniti. All the signs are that Montague made a busy and enthusiastic start to the new season. There soon followed the two occasions when Montague played for Blackheath with Lord Harris. The first time, on 9 June, was against the Royal Artillery: Harris opened the batting with Stanley Christopherson and made 92. The second time was at Bickley Park on 16 June, and again Harris and Christopherson opened the innings. The latter's position was more in deference to his seniority as an England colleague of Lord Harris than to his real batting ability. Montague did not distinguish himself: he took no wickets in either match and scored no runs. If Harris ever realised that he had shared a dressing room and a committee room with a Ripper suspect, he would have been less than pleased. Few would have dared point it out to him.

Around this time Montague's form did decline. The following week, on 23 June, he made another nought, and was not selected for the matches in early July against the Old Wykehamists and the MCC. He belonged to both clubs, and might have expected to play. It was in early July that his mother was finally committed to the Brook Lunatic Asylum at Clapton, and this could have affected his appearances and his form. Still, he was back playing against the Band of Brothers on 14 July – a side that included Lord Harris.

A week later he played his last competitive game for Blackheath. This was against Beckenham at the Rectory Field, where he took 3 wickets and scored 23.

It was noticeable that Montague's form for Blackheath fell away during 1888. He started the season quite well, but from June onwards the runs and wickets dried up, and he may even have been left out of the side. In previous seasons he usually took around 40 wickets and scored 200–300 runs. In 1888 his tally was 18 wickets and 66 runs. All this may have been due to a simple loss of form or it is possible he was distracted by his legal work and his new friends at the Inner Temple. His administrative work for the club did not suffer and he remained an important member of the Committee.

The reason he played no more for Blackheath after 21 July, apart from the club match on 8 September, may not have been primarily due to his mother's condition. In both the previous years it seemed that after the end of the school term he had moved back to Wimborne to spend time on his work as a special pleader. This was always centred on the West Country, and he continued to play cricket for nearby clubs. On 3 and 4 August he played for the Gentlemen of Bournemouth against the Parsees, a visiting Indian touring side. He took 6 wickets. A couple of days later he played for the Gentlemen of Dorset against the same opposition. The following weekend, on 10 and 11 August, he turned out for the Gentlemen of Dorset against Bournemouth at the end of the latter's cricket week. Then on 22 August he appeared for Bournemouth against Sir William Bathurst's XI at Salisbury. He also fitted in a match for Kingston Park. There was no sign his mother's health or anything else was inhibiting his West Country cricket. Ever since the death of her husband, William, three years earlier, Ann Druitt's mental health had steadily worsened. It was sadly inevitable that one day she would have to leave Wimborne, so it cannot have been a shock to Montague when events took their course.

It might be thought that Montague's mother had been placed at Clapton so he, Edward and Georgiana could visit her from their nearby bases. This is improbable, as more of the family were in the Bournemouth and Christchurch area, and family visits were not a feature of life in a lunatic asylum. Grim though these institutions were, they were an improvement from the days when patients were simply locked up in padded cells in workhouses. Then no proper records were kept, and the inmates were not covered by parliamentary legislation. At least the Acts of 1808, 1815 and 1828 meant that the Justices of the Peace could build tailor-made asylums, and in 1831 the first was opened at Hanwell, Middlesex. Yet they always remained utterly charmless, threatening places from which people seldom emerged in better health than when they were admitted.

Ann Druitt's final years must have been uncompromisingly awful. She was moved from asylum to asylum. After two months at Clapton, she went to an institution in Brighton, and on 31 May 1890 to Manor House Asylum, Chiswick. Manor House was by reputation an asylum that looked after middle-class patients and sometimes members of the gentry. It was run by Dr Thomas Seymour Tuke and had capacity for around forty badly disturbed patients with about the same number of staff. The Tukes were a Quaker family whose commitment to the treatment of mental disorders began in the eighteenth century with William Tuke. He was the man who 'struck the chains from lunatics and laid the foundation of all modern humane treatment'. Thomas Tuke was therefore following the family tradition at Manor House. He was also the uncle of the artist Henry Tuke, and it seems that Henry, in respect for Ann Druitt, his uncle's charge, had given a painting to the Druitt family.

Henry Tuke fitted well into the artistic and sporting environments of the late nineteenth century. He was a friend of G.F. Watts, visited James Whistler in Tite Street and painted portraits of W.G. Grace, Spofforth and C.B. Fry. He watched cricket at Lord's in the company of Ranjitsinhji, who bought some large paintings from him. Also among his friends were Lord Ronald Gower, the MP, sculptor and royal courtier, T.E. Lawrence and two prime ministers, Gladstone and Asquith. His subject matter was often unclothed young boys besporting themselves on the beach.

Henry Tuke was the same age as Montague and the same generation as Herbert Druitt, the collector. This may be the connection between the Tukes and the Druitts, and why *The Cabin*

Boy painting came to be at the Red House Museum. In addition there is the possibility that the story about Montague's father taking in unbalanced aristocrats at Westfield House relates to the Tukes' family tradition of mental health treatment, and that William Druitt was handling the overflow from Manor House. Both were doctors, and William had retired from general practice on health grounds. This would be another link between the Tukes and the Druitts. William's initiative would have been prior to his wife's problems, but nevertheless it would explain why Ann ended her days at Manor House.

On 15 December 1890 Ann Druitt died of a heart attack. Fortunately, she was never in a condition to understand the events that would unravel at the end of 1888. There was one strange feature of her stays in confinement. In 1869 the Prince of Wales had been involved in a divorce scandal between Sir Charles and Lady Mordaunt. The usual cover-up took place, and Lady Mordaunt was certified insane and placed in an asylum for the rest of her life. The odd thing was that the Lunacy Commission, set up after the Lunacy Act of 1845, kept regular and individual reports on only about twelve patients out of hundreds throughout the country. On this small list the names of Harriet Mordaunt and Ann Druitt regularly appeared. Years later when Annie Crook, the mother of the Duke of Clarence's daughter, Alice, was kept in Guy's Hospital in South London for five months prior to being declared insane, she was known to the staff as 'Mrs Mordaunt'. This was a black reference to the fact that both women had had affairs with the Prince of Wales. According to Eduardo Zinner, the European editor of *Ripperologist*, it was William Gull who certified Harriet Mordaunt, and Melvyn Fairclough in his book *The Ripper and the Royals* alleges that Gull did the same for Annie Crook. If these claims are correct, Gull was indeed serving the royal family most helpfully.

In the month leading up to the first murder on 31 August, we know that Montague fulfilled a busy cricket schedule. His cricket did not finish at the end of August. On 1 September he played for Canford against Wimborne on Lord Wimborne's ground. Of course it was possible for Montague to have travelled back to Wimborne from Whitechapel in time to play cricket on 1 September. However, the logistics alone make it improbable that he would have interrupted a programme of cricket to travel to London to commit a murder, and then rush back to the cricket field. He would have needed somewhere to clean up and change his clothes. His chambers were not in the immediate vicinity, and anyway the practicalities were such that he could not have used them for this purpose. The rooms at 9 King's Bench Walk were lawyers' offices and business accommodation addresses. There were eight sets of chambers at this address, which were used by two Queen's Counsel, fourteen barristers and two firms of solicitors. The barristers were led by Sir Arthur Richard Jelf QC, a formidable man who became a High Court Judge. He would have allowed into the premises only those men he believed could pay their way and who would observe the rules and traditions of the legal world. To imagine blood-stained clothes could be changed at the chambers, even in the middle of the night, without Jelf getting to hear about it, is not realistic.

The distance between any of the murder sites and 9 King's Bench Walk is also further than may be imagined. By any route it would be about an hour's walk, so for a blood-stained person to cover this distance unnoticed, even at night, is again not believable. Whoever committed the murders had facilities much closer to Whitechapel.

On the following Monday and Tuesday (3 and 4 September), Montague was scheduled to play for the Gentlemen of Dorset against the Gentlemen of Hampshire at Dean Court, Bournemouth, but the match had to be cancelled because Dorset could not raise a side. Montague's next and last appearance on the cricket field was on Saturday, 8 September, at Blackheath in the end-of-season club match. It was entirely understandable that Montague wanted to return to play, and to say goodbye to team-mates until next season. The date was, of course, also that of the second murder, and the closeness of Whitechapel and Blackheath has been highlighted by Montague's accusers. It is much more likely that, far from prowling the East End, he travelled to Blackheath on the Friday and stayed overnight with friends, or possibly with his sister Georgiana and her family at New Cross. He would have returned to them after the game.

ELEVEN

The End of an Innings

The cricket season was over and in late September the Michaelmas term began. There is nothing to suggest that it was not as uneventful as usual, and Montague was able to undertake some legal work. In the middle of September he represented a man called Christopher Power, who was accused of wounding with a knife. Eventually Power was found insane and sent to a lunatic asylum by the judge, Mr Justice Charles. This was the same judge whose celebratory dinner Montague had attended the previous year. Two weeks later on 1 October Montague appeared at another court for an appeal in the West Country. This was the day after the 'Double Event' murders. The next definite news of Montague was when he attended a board meeting of the Blackheath Club on 19 November, ten days after the fifth and last killing. At the meeting he proposed that 'an acre of land be taken behind the grandstand at a similar proportionate rent to that paid for the present land'. There was no sign here, or at a legal meeting three days later, that he was beginning a mental breakdown.

Disaster struck Montague less than two weeks later, on 30 November, when George Valentine dismissed him from his teaching post after eight years for 'serious trouble'. For Montague it must have been cataclysmic. It was completely sudden: there were no warnings, no signs of behavioural changes in Montague and no record of disagreements between himself and Valentine.

What 'serious trouble' meant has never been conclusively established. It could have related to some sort of fraud, or a major row with Valentine. The immediate thought is that he was caught molesting one of the pupils. As the master who covered night-time duties, he had more opportunity than most, yet, if this suggestion is correct, it must surely have been an utterly foolish aberration. Montague had worked for eight years at the school, and George Valentine would have been very alert to any sign that any of his masters were in the slightest way suspect. A scandal of this nature would have led to the closure of the school. If Montague did have these desires, he had always repressed them, as he was bright enough to know that his teaching career and everything he had achieved on the cricket field were dependent on an unblemished reputation. He would have realised that his law career would not withstand any suggestion of paedophilia. At a stroke his network of friends and social contacts, mostly in the world of cricket, would collapse. Also, he would be homeless. He had always given 9 Eliot Place as his main address, and his chambers, too, would cease to be available to him. Even to return to Wimborne might not be an option, as the ownership of Westfield House was by now uncertain. William, his elder brother, may have moved to Bournemouth, the other two brothers had careers elsewhere and Georgiana was married and living in New Cross, which left only the two younger sisters. Besides, an offence of this nature was such that even family members might withdraw their support. It is only guesswork that suggests that Montague's 'serious trouble' related to homosexuality. However, bearing in mind Montague's background of life at boarding school, university, law, cricket, employment at a boys' school and the lack of any record of female relationships, this first thought may be the correct one. Even if it was something less serious, the fact George Valentine had to dismiss him on the spot would have ended his teaching career and his Blackheath cricket connections.

No one ever admitted seeing Montague alive from the time he left the school on Friday, 30 November. On 11 December a friend alerted William that his brother had not been seen for more than a week. When he began enquiries at the school he discovered a note from Montague that read 'since Friday I felt I was going to be like mother, and the best thing for me was to die'. This sounds as if Montague fully appreciated the consequences of what he had done. It was a despairing cry for help. He could see no future.

There may be a significant clue in the motion passed by the Blackheath Cricket Club's directors on 21 December, when the whereabouts of Montague were still unknown. It said: 'The Honorary Secretary and Treasurer, Mr M.J. Druitt, having gone abroad, it was resolved that he be hereby removed from the post of Honorary Secretary and Treasurer.' At first the words 'having gone abroad' sound like a callous euphemism for 'he has gone and good riddance'. In fact, it may have been the truth as the Committee understood it. From George Valentine they might well have known the real reason for Montague's dismissal, and it is possible that Montague had been given one dispensation. In recognition of his work and status at Blackheath, and because up to that moment he had been an entirely popular member of the community, Valentine may have given him the option of leaving the country instead of the police being called.

This option was often used among the upper classes to save them the embarrassment of a court case after scandal broke. The Prince of Wales went to Europe at the time of the Mordaunt divorce, Lord Arthur Somerset and Charles Hammond were allowed to flee to France to avoid the Cleveland Street trial, and Oscar Wilde went to Germany to evade the fallout after the Lord Chamberlain had banned his proposed London production of *Salome*.

This would have starred Sarah Bernhardt: she was another of the Prince of Wales's conquests and was described at some of the more conservative levels of society as 'a woman of notorious character and unashamed hedonism'. Nor was she a person to miss an opportunity. She had learnt of the Prince's patronage of the MCC and had seen the painting by George Barrable and Sir Robert Ponsonby Staples of him standing by the boundary line at Lord's with the Princess of Wales. Moreover, Lillie Langtry was featured among the crowd. It was sufficient for her to proclaim, 'I do love cricket – it's so very English.' All this was clearly too much for the Lord Chamberlain.

Wilde was given the chance to disappear abroad a second time in the hours between his failed case against the Marquis of Queensberry and his arrest under the Labouchere amendment. This short freedom seemed like an invitation to leave for France, but he ignored it and paid the price with two years' hard labour. Ironically, on release he did go to France, perhaps hoping to meet his old friend Henri de Toulouse-Lautrec. Lautrec had included him in his 1892 painting *At the Moulin Rouge*. It hangs in the Veletrzni Palace in Prague. His idea was unsuccessful as by 1898 poor Henri was in a sanatorium and Wilde died in France two years later. Henry Labouchere had been no crusading paragon. Masquerading under the guise of traditional respectability, he was as manipulative as any of the age. Queen Victoria had worked him out: 'that horrible lying Labouchere,' she said. Even the freewheeling Prince of Wales described him as 'a viper'. It has to be said that part of their ire was due to Labouchere's republicanism. At Victoria's funeral he claimed his privileged position in a special stand in the Mall reserved for Lords and MPs and then described the pomp and processions as 'barbaric' and the mood of the crowd as 'cheerful'. This was the man whose bill sent Wilde to prison.

When the Cleveland Street trial loomed in late 1889, it was judicious indeed for the Duke of Clarence and the royal family that the Duke departed from public view by means of an overseas trip. This trip began in 1889 and took in Greece, Egypt and India. He returned in May of the following year when the scandal of the Cleveland Street case was over. Edward Langtry, too, was found an overseas posting when his divorce petition against the Prince of Wales was withdrawn. Sending people abroad was a convenient solution to awkward social problems.

Montague was of sufficient standing and erstwhile popularity to be given this opportunity. Valentine also knew that to invite a police investigation would be a disaster for the school. As there had been no sightings of Montague up to 21 December, the Committee may have believed that he had gone abroad. In fact, this was not the case. The truth was far worse.

On 31 December Montague's body was pulled from the Thames off Chiswick Mall, just yards from Harry Wilson's house The Osiers.

The first report of Montague's death appeared in the *County of Middlesex Independent* on Wednesday, 2 January 1889.

FOUND IN THE RIVER: The body of a well dressed man was discovered on Monday in the river off Thorneycroft's torpedo works, by a waterman named Winslow. The police were communicated with and the deceased was conveyed to the mortuary. The body, which is that of a man about 40 years of age, has been in the water about a month. From certain papers found on the body friends at Bournemouth have been telegraphed to. An inquest will be held today.

The original coroner's report no longer exists, but there was a long account of the inquest in the *Acton, Chiswick and Turnham Green Gazette*, dated 5 January 1889.

FOUND DROWNED. – Shortly after midday on Monday, a Waterman named Winslade of Chiswick found the body of a man, well-dressed, floating in the Thames off Thorneycroft's. He at once informed a constable, and without delay the body was conveyed on the ambulance to the mortuary. On Wednesday afternoon, Dr Diplock, coroner, held the inquest at the Lamb Tap, when the following evidence was adduced: William H. Druitt said he lived in Bournemouth, and that he was a solicitor. The deceased was his brother, who was 31 last birthday. He was a barrister-at-law, and an assistant master in a school in Blackheath. He had stayed with witness at Bournemouth for a night towards the end of October. Witness had heard from a friend on the 11th December that deceased had not been heard of at his chambers for more than a week. Witness then went to London to make inquiries, and at Blackheath he found that deceased had got into serious trouble at the school, and had been dismissed. That was on 30 December. Witness had deceased's things searched where he resided, and found a paper addressed to him (produced). The coroner read this letter, which was to the effect: 'Since Friday I felt that I was going to be like mother, and the best thing for me was to die.'

Witness continuing, said deceased had never made any Attempt on his life before. His mother became insane in July Last. He had no other relative. Henry Winslade was the next Witness. He said that he lived at No. 4, Shore Street, Paxton Road, and that he was a waterman. About one o'clock on Monday he was on the river in a boat, when he saw the body Floating. The tide was at half flood running up. He brought the body ashore and gave information to the police. PC George Moulson, 216 T 131, said he searched the body, which was fully dressed, excepting the hat and collar. He found four large stones in each pocket in the top coat; £2.10s in gold, 7s in silver, 2d in bronze, two cheques on the London and Provincial Bank (one for £50 and the other for £16), a first class season ticket from Blackheath to London (South Western Railway), a second-half return Hammersmith to Charing Cross (dated 1 December), a silver watch, gold chain with silver guinea attached, a pair of kid gloves, and a white handkerchief. There were no papers or letters of any kind. There were no marks of injury on the body, but it was rather decomposed. A verdict of suicide while in unsound mind was returned.

There are several discrepancies in this report of the inquest, and perhaps the inquest itself was less than thorough. The report in the *Gazette* says that 'no papers or letters were found on the body', whereas the *Independent* refers to 'certain papers found on the body'. In the report of the inquest there is no mention of medical evidence, which would have been needed to establish cause and time of death. Nor was there any effort to report who was the last person to see Montague alive, nor any mention of George Valentine. Valentine would have been a key witness to establish Montague's mental state and his reaction to dismissal. The report records a dismissal date of 30 December, which is an error for 30 November. Nor did the journals agree on the name of the waterman who found the body. More importantly, William Druitt is alleged to have said that Montague had no other relative. This is untrue, and it would be extraordinary for a solicitor to lie under oath in a matter that could be so easily exposed. Montague had two other living brothers, three sisters, a mother, albeit in an asylum, and several cousins. The 'since Friday' letter produced by him was read in full by the coroner, so the twenty-one words recorded by the reporter were only a part of it. When the letter was found among Montague's possessions at the school, it is not certain if it was addressed to William or George Valentine. In any event, either the report was carelessly written or the inquest itself was perfunctory. It may be wrong to blame the *Gazette* entirely. The inquest may have been instructed to avoid involving Valentine and to gloss over how Montague had spent his last hours and with whom he had been. These omissions could have been made because a copy of the report on Montague's death had to be sent to the Home Office and a full report could have included some sensitive names. There was no sign at the inquest that William made any attempt to get these basic questions addressed, which could have avoided the considerable stigma to the family of a verdict of suicide. He was a solicitor and he knew which questions to ask. He may have been nervous to have too many boulders turned over. His supine attitude suggests a suicide verdict suited him quite well. Perhaps the person to read the report at the Home Office with most interest was Evelyn Ruggles-Brise. Memories of cricket field rivalry at Winchester and Oxford would have been especially poignant, and the damage done to his university cricket career by Montague could have seemed less important.

The manner of Montague's supposed suicide is most improbable. If he wished to die, there were parts of the Thames much closer to Blackheath, and the Embankment is only a matter of yards from the

Inner Temple. It is also statistically unusual to commit suicide by drowning, especially in the middle of the winter. Furthermore Montague was a good swimmer. There had been swimming pools at Winchester and George Valentine's school, so for him to choose to kill himself in this way makes little sense.

It is possible to try to reconstruct Montague's last hours. If he was faced with the ultimatum to go abroad, he would have had to leave immediately, and there would have been no one he could have turned to in Blackheath. One source of help and encouragement could have been Harry Wilson's chummery at Chiswick Mall. Montague had never been abroad, and the prospect would have been overwhelmingly daunting. At least he would not have needed a passport or an identity card. He could have travelled abroad without any sort of official permission and could have changed his money without restriction as passports were not introduced until 1914. But Montague would have needed advice and perhaps a 'safe house' to stay at for a couple of days so he could change his assets into cash. He would also have needed the names and addresses of people on the continent who could have helped him. He would not have expected the clientele of The Osiers to be too critical of his misdemeanour, whatever it was.

Such a plan would account for his smart dress and the large sums of money (worth over £3,000 in today's values) that were found on his body. The cheques were almost certainly severance pay from the school. Any suitcases could have been either at The Osiers or at a London main-line station. The return half of his Charing Cross to Hammersmith train ticket confirms his intention to go back to Central London. Hammersmith station is only a few minutes' walk from The Osiers.

His plan may have collapsed if his reception was less than warm. Montague was not an Apostle, perhaps not a frequent visitor to The Osiers and not a senior member of that group. The regulars' sense of self-protection would have been alerted, and Montague could have been seen as a threat to their security. Perhaps he was rebuffed. In the insidious way of society closing ranks, perhaps he was advised that the only honourable solution to his problem was suicide.

Montague would have known too much of the antics of the Duke of Clarence, the goings-on at the Cleveland Street Club, and the nefarious underworld that existed among the Victorian gentry. Potentially he could have blackmailed them. It would have suited them for Montague to be dead, and if Montague could be conveniently persuaded to kill himself, the threat that he may have been perceived to represent to the royal family and some of the Victorian nobility would be dealt with.

It is also possible that Montague could have been murdered. There are two potential theories. Montague could have become a liability at The Osiers. Perhaps matters at the chummery took a nasty turn if Montague would not cooperate, and some members took fright. They could have drugged and overcome Montague and either put him into the Thames, with pockets weighted, to drown, or thrust him into a culvert to be released into the Thames a few weeks later or washed out by a 'half flood tide running up'.

A second murder theory concerns the role of his brother William. William was the eldest son, the head of the household and legal executor of the family estate. His father was dead and it would have been with William's permission that his mother entered Brook Asylum. This meant she had no legal control over the estate. William wished to wind this up to his own advantage, but Montague, as a barrister, stood in his way. He also knew that Montague had substantial assets but no will, so he would be the beneficiary. At the same time William was investing heavily in property and land in the Bournemouth area. He, therefore, had the motive and could have set about organising Montague's death. It was William who first used the phrase 'serious trouble', and this may have been a carefully chosen comment to mislead observers into the wrong conclusion. If William had such a plan, it worked. On 24 July 1891 he was granted letters of administration for Montague's estate valued at £1,500. These letters included the sentence: 'Ann Druitt, widow, the natural and lawful mother and only next of kin of the said intestate (Montague Druitt) having survived him, but died without taking upon herself letters of administration of his personal estate'.

Furthermore, ten days earlier on 14 July, William had been granted, by the same legal procedure, ownership of his mother's estate worth £2,419. She had died in December 1890. Had William planned this a couple of years earlier and had his mother committed and Montague murdered? If so, he had succeeded to the tune of £4,000, or about £200,000 today. His passive behaviour at the inquest would make sense. Even Montague's seven shares, which he owned in the Blackheath Club, passed to William after his death, as the club's transfer of shares book shows.

The idea that William Druitt was working to a plan to bring all the family assets to himself is strengthened by his actions immediately after his mother's death. Within six months of being granted letters of administration he had sold Westfield House to Colonel Sir William Watts. Sir William was from a prominent Bournemouth family, and had been commander of the 3rd Battalion Welsh Regiment. He served extensively in South Africa. He was also Deputy Provincial Grand Master of Dorsetshire Freemasons, and had been a contemporary of Francis Lacey at Sherborne School. It is quite likely his family had been friends of the Druitts long before he bought Westfield House.

William Druitt died in 1909 and by that time had accumulated assets worth over £1 million by today's values. This was left to his younger brother Arthur and a cousin James. Unusually, he left nothing to his brother Edward, who as a career soldier was not wealthy. It begs the question of whether there had been a serious family disagreement at some stage.

Montague's passing was noted in the local newspaper. The *Hampshire Advertiser* dated 12 January 1889 included a brief tribute and account of the funeral.

SAD DEATH OF A BARRISTER

An inquiry was held last week by Mr Diplock, at Chiswick, respecting the death of Montague John Druitt, 31 years of age, who was found drowned in the Thames. The deceased was identified by his brother, Mr Wm Harvey Druitt, a solicitor residing at Bournemouth who stated that the deceased was a barrister-at-law, but had lately been an assistant at a school at Blackheath. The deceased had left a letter, addressed to Mr Valentine, of the school, in which he alluded to suicide. Evidence having been given as to discovering deceased in the Thames – upon him was found a cheque for £50 and £16 in gold – the jury returned a verdict of suicide while of 'unsound mind'. The deceased gentleman was well-known and much respected in this neighbourhood. The funeral took place in Wimborne Cemetery on Thursday afternoon, and the body was followed to the grave by deceased's relatives and a few friends, including Mr W.H. Druitt, Mr Arthur Druitt, Revd C.H. Druitt, Mr J. Druitt, sen., Mr J. Druitt, jun., Mr J.T. Homer, and Mr Wyke-Smith. The funeral service was read by the Vicar of the Minster, Wimborne, the Revd F.J. Huyshe, assisted by the Revd W.E. Plater.

There were some conspicuous absentees from the ceremony. None of Montague's sisters was present, nor was his brother Edward, nor were any representatives of his life in Blackheath. Mr Homer and Mr Wyke-Smith were old family friends. Matilda Jane Druitt, Montague's cousin, noted in her diary:

Wednesday 2 Jan. Heard of Montie Druitt's death. Mrs Maberly and Oswald called. Another rehearsal at school.
Thursday 3 Jan. Herbert and I went to Mr Argyle's funeral. James went to Wimborne with Jim to attend Montie's funeral. Scenes from Pilgrims Progress acted by Maud and others at School.

These were hardly grief-stricken entries. Montague's death rated no more highly than the visits of friends or some play rehearsals. The funeral of a family friend took precedence, but perhaps the circumstances of Montague's death meant the family wanted his funeral to be as quiet as possible. Before, Montague had been an integral part of the family, and he regularly exchanged correspondence and socialised with his uncles and cousins. The previous year he had visited a relation in Norfolk with Matilda. The funeral must have been a small, sad and very private occasion.

In fact, Montague was fortunate to be buried with due dignity in Wimborne cemetery alongside his father and his friend Nicholas 'Felix' Wanostrocht. In those days suicide was a crime, and someone committing suicide could not be buried in consecrated ground unless the words 'of unsound mind' were included in the coroner's verdict. Furthermore, Montague was laid to rest in the more privileged part of Wimborne Cemetery. This is divided by a path into two burial areas: the left side of the path is kept for Anglicans, and the right for all others, described collectively as Nonconformists. Montague lies on the left. A slightly surprising aspect of the funeral was its cost. Sometime after the funeral, the cemetery superintendent recalled that the usual price for a grave was about 8s (40p), but Montague's had cost £5 11s. Perhaps this included the large stone cross on a double plinth that stands in the churchyard to this day. Montague's name is still legible.

No obituaries appeared in the local Blackheath press, in contrast to his fellow team-mate and schoolmaster Frederick Lacey. Lacey died aged 38 in 1890, and the local newspaper carried a report. Although Lacey replaced Montague as a club director, Montague had held senior posts in the club for longer and had seen the club through a critical period and hence was a more significant figure in Blackheath society. The only possible explanation is that his death and its circumstances were hushed up. At a board meeting of the Blackheath Club on 7 February 1889 a tribute was paid to Montague: 'It was resolved that the Directors had heard with much regret of the death of M.J. Druitt who had zealously fulfilled the duties of Honorary Secretary and Treasurer for three and a half years.' It was hardly an adequate tribute to someone who had played for the club with enormous enthusiasm and much skill for eight years and who had served on the Committee for nearly all that time.

In retrospect, Montague can be seen as one of the founders of the modern Blackheath Club, which is still based on the Rectory Field grounds for which he negotiated over 100 years ago. A few years later in 1893 the then Secretary, Malcolm Christopherson, referred to the contribution made by Montague as a player and administrator in an article about the history of the Blackheath Cricket Club.

The annual report for 1888 recorded Montague's playing contribution in the averages but was published too early to take his death into account. The 1889 report ignored Montague altogether, which can only have been deliberate, since it was usual to pay tribute to deceased club members who had held administrative posts. For example, in the 1890 Annual Report both Frederick Lacey and G.W. Burton who had died that year were generously mentioned.

Exactly 100 years after his death, Montague did receive a tribute of sorts that he might have appreciated. David Frith's book *By His Own Hand* is a survey of those cricketers who have committed suicide. A description of Montague's death is included in the chapter 'Eminent Victorians'. Also in the chapter are accounts of the sad demises of Andrew Stoddart, Arthur Shrewsbury, Albert Trott and William Scotton. All these men were extremely good Test players. There is a secondary chapter, 'More Victorians', which deals with lesser players. At least Montague had been classified with the most famous.

TWELVE

Gaylords

In the words of Lord Alfred Douglas, the lover and ruin of Oscar Wilde, the club at 19 Cleveland Street existed to facilitate 'the love that dare not speak its name'. For several years the club had been owned and run by Charles Hammond to provide services, ostensibly, for leading members of society. In reality it was used by any man who could afford a guinea for half an hour's entertainment. It was, in short, a homosexual brothel.

This became so flagrantly clear to the world at large that the police were eventually moved to action. For a long time the activities of the club had been ignored by the hierarchy, some of whom were eager customers, but the nature of the business was so far beyond the law that action had to be taken. It was, after all, only in 1861 that the death penalty for buggery had been withdrawn, but it was still punishable by life imprisonment. Elementary traps were set for Telegraph boys working from the nearby Central Post Office, and it was not long before a case could be made to convince the Director of Public Prosecutions to act. Even then certain individuals within the police and the government procrastinated, but eventually the case was heard and the club closed.

The closure of the club in 1889 came too late to interest Montague. It is not certain if he ever went to the club, but it would be surprising if among the Cleveland Street membership there were not a few Apostles such as Harry Wilson and James Stephen. The Duke of Clarence was certainly a member. This has been established from membership lists. On the Department of Public Prosecution's file of patrons the Duke is referred to as P.A.V. (Prince Albert Victor). The equerry to the Duke's father and manager of the royal stables, Lord Arthur Somerset ('Call me "Podge"'), and Lord Euston were frequent visitors.

The influence of the clientele meant that for a long time the club could evade any threats to its business. It offered a menu of homosexual and transvestite services: Guardsmen, labourers and Telegraph boys were available on request. The charge for a Telegraph boy was a guinea, of which the boy kept four shillings (20p). Eventually a boy was arrested carrying a suspiciously large amount of cash. He was questioned about a robbery and admitted the source of the money. Lord Somerset's name was to the fore. Prosecution and conviction eventually followed, and the ringleader at the Post Office, George Veck, received four months in jail. Veck had been masquerading as a clergyman, and his sentence was derisory. A vicar found guilty of a similar charge a year earlier had been jailed for life.

The say-so of the club members reached the judiciary itself. Before the trial Charles Hammond was given free passage to the continent, and Lord Somerset was allowed to escape to France and then on to Constantinople. The defence's solicitor, Arthur Newton, organised the cover-up and arranged for the boys to be sent off to Australia. Each received £20, a pound a week for three years and a new suit. One of the boys, Algernon Alleys, was told: 'The reason we want to get you away is so you should not give evidence against you know who.' It was Alleys who had received indecent letters from a 'Mr Brown', who was none other than Lord Somerset. Another dignitary said to be involved was Sir William Jervois, a man of military and colonial background who at the time of the trial had recently returned from twelve years' service in Australia. At one time he had been in charge of the London district of the Royal Engineers. Arthur Newton continued his somewhat flamboyant career by acting for the defence in the Oscar Wilde trial and appearing for Dr Crippen. He was eventually struck off for fraud, and finished up as a prison librarian at Parkhurst jail.

The trial was not 'a little local difficulty', it was of major international interest. The *Marlborough Express* in New Zealand, free of UK press restrictions, reported the scandal in clear terms. Under the headline 'A London Club Scandal – the Affair Suppressed' the report read:

> A horrible scandal with a private West End club is reported. Ninety eight members in all are implicated. Thirty one warrants have been issued, but will not be executed on the under-standing that the persons connected with it leave the United Kingdom. The list of offenders includes future dukes, the sons of dukes, peers, Hebrew financiers, many honourable persons, and several officers of the Imperial Army. All the matter [*sic*] have suddenly resigned their commissions. The offenders have fled. The newspapers have suppressed reference to the scandal, but there is no doubt of its having taken place.

New Zealand was a long way to go to find out what was going on.

The real success of the Establishment was to keep the Duke of Clarence's name out of the trial, although the public were not fooled.

There was more to Cleveland Street than just one club. It stood on the edge of the artistic Fitzrovia area. Between 1882 and 1886 Walter Sickert had a studio at No. 15, and it was here that the Duke of Clarence visited Sickert. A few years earlier William Holman Hunt and Dante Rossetti – leading members of the Pre-Raphaelite Brotherhood – had worked together at No. 7. Another inhabitant of the area who appeared on the margins of the Ripper story was Winifred Collis. She was a housemaid at No. 27 and stayed with her old friend Mary Kelly in Whitechapel a matter of days before Kelly's murder. One way or another there was a lot going on in Cleveland Street in the 1880s.

Just round the corner from Cleveland Street was the Hundred Guineas Club in Nassau Street. The name was also the annual subscription, around £5,000 today. Montague could never have paid a membership fee that represented half his annual salary. The club specialised in transvestism, but after 2.00 a.m. the staff were instructed to oblige customers with any service required. The Duke of Clarence was a member here too, and in accordance with club rules had to use a woman's name. His was Victoria. 19 Cleveland Street has long since disappeared. Early in the twentieth century some street names were altered, and the site became No. 75. More recently this too has gone, replaced by hospital apartments, but Nassau Street remains much the same. It still has neat Georgian terraced houses protected by black railings. Near the end of Nassau Street is the Gaylord restaurant, probably not named for historical or nostalgic reasons but even so resonant of another era.

The two clubs were by no means the only places which provided such facilities. Oscar Wilde often went to W. Jones's Supper Rooms, which because of its proximity to the Houses of Parliament was popular with certain MPs. Similarly the Crown, the Pakenham and the Windsor Castle, all public houses in central London, were meeting places for like-minded men. Also favoured were the Cremorne Gardens and the Midnight clubs.

Oscar Wilde knew all about 19 Cleveland Street, and it was noticed that his behaviour was more 'circumspect' during and after the trial. The *Scots Observer* wrote pointedly: 'If Mr Wilde can write for none but outlawed noblemen and perverted telegraph boys, the sooner he takes to tailoring (or some other decent trade) the better for his own reputation and public morals.' This was a direct reference to the Cleveland Street trial, and to the flight of his friend, Lord Arthur Somerset.

The Duke of Clarence was thoroughly at home in such environments, and no doubt a popular participant. As an individual, however, he could scarcely have been less distinguished or less interesting company. He had little ability to learn anything. When he joined the 10th Hussars, a regiment to this day referred to in the investigative tabloid press as 'the raunchy regiment', he could not manage the drill; when he visited France to get to grips with the language, he got no further than the Paris clubs. His entry to Trinity College, Cambridge was on condition he would take no exams and would be awarded an honorary degree. Julian Champkin, writing in the *Mail on Sunday*, summed him up nicely: 'he was very dim, even by royal standards.' Paul Begg, the author, considered him 'an upper-class twit. Lazy and backward to the point of idiocy'.

From the start of his life the omens for the Duke were not good. He was christened Albert Victor Christian Edward but liked to be known as Prince Edward. This was not propitious. Since the early fourteenth century the royal Edwards have had problems. Edward II, a rampant homosexual, was murdered on the orders of his wife in 1327 by having a burning stake thrust up his backside in Berkeley Castle. Edward III presided over the Black Death, which killed one person in three. His eldest son, another Edward, became known as the Black Prince and concocted a treaty with Pedro the Cruel of Spain. He never became king as he predeceased his father. Edward IV arranged for the private execution in the Tower in 1478 of an earlier Duke of Clarence by having him drowned in a vat of malmsey wine. That same Duke of Clarence had ordered a banquet for 10,000 guests and served thirty courses. Four hundred years later his namesake would have approved. Edward IV died in 1483 'worn out by his debaucheries'. According to a Channel 4 programme in January 2004, Edward IV was illegitimate. It claimed he was conceived following an affair his mother had with a bowman at a time when his assumed father, Richard of York, was away in France for several months. This illegitimacy could invalidate the claim to the monarchy of every subsequent British sovereign. However, the official view is that Richard was accompanied by his wife Cecily to France in 1441 and Edward was born in April 1442 in Rouen.

Edwards V and VI had brief, unhappy lives: Edward V was one of the Little Princes murdered in the Tower, and Edward VI, the only son of Henry VIII, died at 15 of consumption. The grisly record continued with Edward VII, the Duke of Clarence's father, who attracted public outcry by his womanising and profligacy. Thus a royal name containing 'Edward' or 'Clarence' was risky, and the Duke of Clarence had them both. Matters did not improve in the twentieth century with the traitorous Edward VIII. If the present Prince Charles is at all superstitious he might not have been entirely happy about moving into a home called Clarence House.

As a sportsman the Duke was consistently incompetent. Even his official biographer James Vincent struggled to be kind. He wrote that 'in the athletic world the Prince was no very prominent person'. Despite being a member of MCC he never played cricket, nor had any interest in the game. This may have been a relief to the MCC committee for had the Duke wished to play it would have had to be at Lord's. His grandfather Prince Albert became a patron of the club in 1847 and his father twenty years later. It was the Duke's father who had been the largest contributor to the fund to buy the freehold of the ground, so the MCC would never have refused the Duke a game, no matter how great the embarrassment. The Duke's only contribution to the game of cricket was to lay the foundation stone for the new pavilion at the Melbourne Cricket Ground on 2 July 1881. For this service he and his brother were made members and each received a silver trowel. He performed this duty during a visit to Melbourne when he was on his world cruise on HMS *Bacchante*, accompanied by his guardian, Canon John Dalton. Dalton was another of the Duke's friends who would have been at home in the Cleveland Club.

The Duke tried football, rowing, riding, lacrosse, lawn tennis and hockey with no success. Theo Aronson in his book *Prince Eddy and the Homosexual Underworld* records that his favourite pastime was 'a pleasant summer evening with a friend upon the water among the beautiful surroundings of the Backs'. He would have shared the view that Oscar Wilde expressed when asked which outdoor athletics he preferred: 'I am afraid I play no outdoor games at all. Except dominoes. I have sometimes played dominoes outside French cafés.' Quite possibly the Duke developed this talent during his sojourn to learn the language. However, the story that the Duke set a fashion in slip-on shoes because he could not tie laces is not true.

The Duke did not confine himself to all-male company: he consorted regularly with prostitutes. At Bonhams in March 2002 two letters from the Duke were auctioned for over £8,000. They were written in 1890 and 1891 and were to his solicitor, George Lewis, about paying off two prostitutes with whom he had become involved. He wrote: 'I am very pleased that you are able to settle with Miss Richardson, although £200 is rather expensive for letters. I presume there is no other way of getting them back. I will also do all I can to get back the one or two letters written to the other lady.' This predicament encapsulates the Duke's naivety. George Lewis was famed for extracting society figures from awkward situations, and was known especially for his services to the royal family. It was this work that earned him a knighthood in 1892.

In 1891 the Duke became engaged to Princess May of Teck, but when he died suddenly the following year she moved on to his younger brother George. She eventually became Queen Mary.

Not even the death of the Duke, possibly from pneumonia, was clear cut. There was, and remains, a strong belief that the royal family had him removed from view because of his incompetence and licentiousness. Many believed that the 13th Earl of Strathmore allowed the Duke to be hidden away in his Scottish retreat, Glamis Castle, for the rest of his days. In return the Earl's family was promised a significant marriage into royalty. This happened when the Earl's granddaughter Elizabeth Bowes-Lyon married the man who became George VI. Patrick Bowes-Lyon, son of the 13th Earl of Strathmore, had been one of a group of young men which had close associations with the Apostles. He was the only aristocrat to travel with the Duke on HMS *Bacchante* in 1879. He also shared a room with the Duke at Trinity College, and later the two frequently dined together at the Middle Temple, so it was probably Patrick Bowes-Lyon's idea to use Glamis Castle as a hideaway. Glamis had been in the family since 1372 and has always been a forbidding place. It was the backdrop for Shakespeare's *Macbeth*, and it is, by repute, the most haunted castle in Scotland. It would not be the first time, nor the last, that inconvenient royals were made to disappear by one means or another.

There is a story that links the Duke uncomfortably with the Ripper crimes. It came to light in 1973 when Joseph Sickert, son of the Victorian artist Walter Sickert, claimed the murders were a device to cover up what would have been a most controversial relationship for the Duke. Soon afterwards, Stephen Knight repeated Sickert's story in his book *Jack the Ripper: The Final Solution*. However, Sickert was somewhat temperamental: he denied the story in 1978, and then in 1991 restated and embellished the tale to Melvyn Fairclough for his book *The Ripper and the Royals*. The story remains unproven yet the essence of it is tantalisingly possible, and Theo Aronson thought it worthwhile to give it prominence in his book.

Apparently in 1884 James Stephen introduced the Duke to his cousin, Annie Elizabeth Crook, who lived at 6 Cleveland Street across the road from the club. She worked in a tobacco and confectionery shop at 22 Cleveland Street owned by a Mrs Morgan, herself a witness at the Cleveland Street trial. There is still a shop at this address today although now it sells buckles and buttons. Annie Crook shared her home with a West End prostitute, Mary Kelly. Kelly worked in a gay club for gentlemen in the West End, and, in view of her address, this was probably the Cleveland. On 18 April 1885 Annie Crook bore the Duke of Clarence a daughter. She was called Alice Margaret, and her birth certificate still exists. It shows she was born at Marylebone Workhouse and that her mother was Annie Elizabeth Crook, whose residence was 6 Cleveland Street, Fitzroy Square. The name of the father was left blank. Mary Kelly became her nanny. In 1886, 6 Cleveland Street was demolished and Kelly left to resume her old trade in the East End. She, of course, knew the full story of Alice Margaret's parentage. Three more names had been added to the eclectic list of Cleveland Street regulars, so many of whom had a part to play in each other's lives.

In November 1888 Kelly became the Ripper's fifth victim. There may have been a previous attempt to kill Mary Kelly in September when Catherine Eddowes was murdered by mistake. Mary Kelly anticipated her fate. At her inquest her boyfriend Joseph Barnett was asked if Kelly ever seemed frightened. 'Yes several times,' he replied, and went on to say that he had 'bought newspapers and I read to her everything about the murders'. Chief Inspector Walter Dew confirmed this evidence. He said, 'There was no woman in the whole of Whitechapel more frightened of Jack the Ripper than Marie Kelly.'

THIRTEEN

'Curiouser and curiouser'

The value of Montague's assets on his death has been a source of comment. £1,500 was a large sum to have been acquired by a schoolmaster who had needed the support of his father a few years earlier. The amount was close to his gross earnings in eight years at Valentine's school. An advertisement placed in *The Times* by George Valentine in the April following Montague's death for an assistant master to teach Mathematics and English offered an annual salary of £150 plus board and lodging. Neither can his special pleading work have accounted for much of this. As has been mentioned, the value of the pictures left to Montague in his father's will were a possible source of the money. It is unlikely that he had some sort of fraud in operation relating to his work at the school or as Treasurer of the Cricket Club.

One person who appears to have behaved very nervously on Montague's death is his brother Edward. By 1889 he was an officer in the Royal Engineers and it seems he took fright at the innuendo surrounding Montague. He did not attend the funeral, and immediately put in for a transfer to Australia. The issue of *Cricket* dated 21 February 1889 says under the section 'Pavilion Gossip': 'I notice that Captain E. Druitt of the Royal Engineers has been ordered to place himself in readiness to proceed to Queensland for employment in connection with the Queensland Defence Forces.' This was rather odd, as there had been no British garrison in Australia since 1870. Nevertheless, he stayed in Australia until 1893, and while he was out there met up with his cousin Lionel.

Suspicions about Montague, which did not come to light until long after his death, can be traced back to 1890, although the main rumour was always of doubtful provenance. Lionel was four years older than Montague, and for a short while in 1879 had had his medical practice in the Minories on the edge of the East End. It was sometimes suggested that Montague could have used this address as a base for the murders. However, Lionel had vacated the premises long before the autumn of 1888. Indeed, he had emigrated to Australia in 1886, and never returned to England. Very soon he met and married an Australian, Susan Murray, and they had three daughters, Susan, Isabella and Dorothy. He died in Victoria in 1908.

The year after Edward had met Lionel in Australia, a pamphlet or article appeared that was subsequently attributed to Lionel Druitt entitled 'The East End Murderer – I Knew Him'. It was alleged to have been printed privately by someone called Mr Fell of Dandenong, a suburb of Melbourne. Lionel cannot have known much about the murders, as he was in Australia during 1888, but his information could have been supplied by Edward. No copy of this document was ever found, no matter how many times the State and National Libraries in Australia were checked, and no matter how many professional researchers, writers and amateur sleuths visited the area.

In the early 1960s Daniel Farson, the writer, claimed to have been contacted by someone who had seen the leaflet, but the material was stolen before he could investigate further. Farson visited Melbourne and the Dandenong area and searched exhaustively but found nothing. Despite the lack of evidence, the story persisted.

It was nearly 100 years after the beginning of the story that Martin Howells and Keith Skinner in their 1985 book *The Ripper*

Legacy finally exposed 'The East End Murderer' document as having nothing to do with Edward, or Lionel or Montague. Nor was it of any use in finding the real murderer, although Howells and Skinner did an immense amount of thorough research to trace its source. With the help of local historical societies, in particular those at Dandenong and Kooweerup, the document was finally revealed to be an enclosure for the *St Arnaud Mercury* dated 29 November 1890. It was written by a landlady from the East End of London who claimed to have rented a room to a man who said he was Jack the Ripper.

The article was remembered when, about eighteen months later, an English émigré called Frederick Deeming was arrested in 1892. Deeming had murdered his wife and four children in England before fleeing to Australia with his second wife. He then killed this wife in Melbourne, and was hanged on 23 May at the same jail as Ned Kelly. While in prison he claimed to have been the Ripper, which, although very unlikely, did create much publicity and excitement. On 8 April the *Melbourne Evening Standard* ran the headline 'Jack the Ripper: Deeming at Aldgate on the night of the Whitechapel murders'. Eight days later the *Illustrated Police News* headlined a story on its front page 'Is Deeming Jack the Ripper?' The stories came to nothing, but it was these reports that renewed interest in the landlady's words. Two other key points that connected the Druitt name with Australia were that Deeming used an alias, Mr Drewen (near enough to Druitt for confusion), and that Lionel Druitt had premises in St Arnaud between July 1890 and March 1891. This was simply a coincidence. The article itself had no validity, and was no more than an opportunist piece of fiction, although Scotland Yard was sufficiently interested in Deeming to request a death mask, and this still remains in its Black Museum.

If Montague had gone to The Osiers for help in December 1888, there were several reasons why his reception might have been less than welcoming. With his cricketing commitments during the summer, and his schoolmastering and legal duties, he would not have found time to be more than an infrequent visitor. He was also not a member of two important clubs. Although Montague socialised with many people who were Apostles, he was on the margins. His education, talent for debate, and his affability suggest that he could have achieved election, had he had the key qualification of a Cambridge education. Occasionally undergraduates from elsewhere were admitted to the society, but this was rare. As it was he remained, in the terminology of the Apostles, an 'embryo'.

The second and more important club that he had failed to join was the Freemasons. Had he done so there would have been an obligation on behalf of his fellow members to help him. Freemasonry is always mentioned in the Ripper story, since so many of the people closely or loosely associated with it were masons. One of the reasons why Lord Somerset could escape the Cleveland Street scandal was because of his close friendship with the Duke of Clarence, and his freemasonry connections. He was a member of the same Royal Alpha Lodge as the Duke.

The most famous Ripper incident that may have related to freemasonry concerned Sir Charles Warren, who in 1886 had been appointed Metropolitan Police Commissioner. It was during his term in office that four of the Whitechapel murders occurred. Warren was a keen mason. He had set up the Quatuor Coronati Lodge No. 2076 in 1884, and he knew all about the customs, rituals and codes of freemasonry. Close to the murdered body of the fourth victim, Catherine Eddowes, a message was chalked on a wall: 'The Juwes are The Men That Will not be Blamed for nothing.' This was immediately reported to Warren as a piece of significant evidence that should at least be photographed. At first the word 'Juwes' was thought to relate to the Jews, as it meant Jews in medieval English and was close to the French word for Jews. There was a large Jewish population in the East End and anti-Semitism was commonplace. However, Warren may have assumed a different meaning of the word, for in masonic lore it referred to the three men who murdered Hiram Abiff, the Masonic Grand Master and builder of Solomon's temple. Their names were Jubela, Jubelum and Jubelo, and they were collectively known by the word 'Juwes'. They were executed by a combination of throat cutting, mutilation and removal of body parts.

Montague Druitt as a student at Oxford, *c.* 1879.
(*Provost and Fellows of Winchester College*)

Left: William Druitt, Montague's father. *(Red House Museum)*

Right: Edward Druitt, Montague's younger brother, seated second from the left centre row in the Royal Engineers XI, 1887. *(The Royal Engineers)*

Left: William Harvey Druitt, Montague's elder brother. *(The Red House Museum)*

Opposite, left: Lionel Druitt, Montague's cousin, who emigrated to Australia. *(The Red House Museum)*

Opposite, right: James Druitt senior, uncle of Montague, who attended his funeral. *(The Red House Museum)*

Blair   Pilcher   Renny-Tailyour   Young   Old Thompson
Druitt   Dembleton   W. Strafford   Stafford
Von Donop   Hedley   Friend

Westfield House, Wimborne, where Montague was born and brought up. *(A.A. Leighton)*

Below, left: Ridding Gate, Winchester College, named after the Headmaster, George Ridding. It leads through to the playing fields known as Ridding Field. *(D.J. Leighton) Right:* Alfred Shaw, who took the MCC field against Montague. He was later to bowl the first ball in Test cricket. *(Elliott and Fry)*

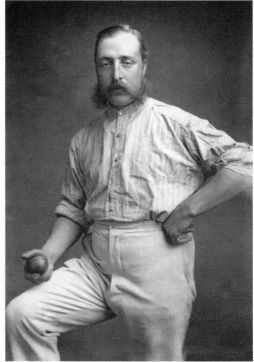

From photo lent by the Rev. J. T. Bramston.

WINCHESTER XI., 1876.

	J. A. Fort.		A. H. Rooper.		F. S. Baines.	W. H. B. Bird.
W. R. Sheldon.		S. J. Wilson.		W. A. Thornton.	J. Eyre.	A. W Moon.
			R. B. A. Prichard.			M. J. Druitt.

The Winchester XI, 1876. Montague is seated bottom right. *(Provost and Fellows of Winchester College)*

The Eton XI, 1876. Of particular interest are Kynaston Studd, Evelyn Ruggles-Brise, Henry Goodhart and Ivo Bligh. *(Provost and Fellows of Eton College)*

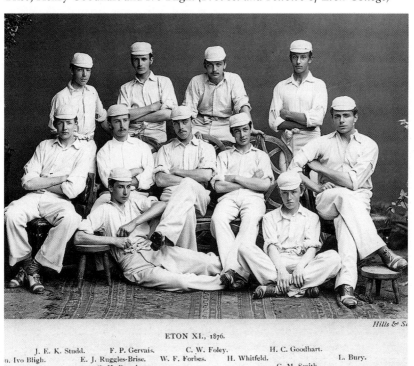

Hills & S

ETON XI., 1876.

	J. E. K. Studd.	F. P. Gervais.		C. W. Foley.		H. C. Goodhart.	
n. Ivo Bligh.		E. J. Ruggles-Brise.	W. F. Forbes.		H. Whitfeld.		L. Bury.
		G. H. Portal.			C. M. Smith.		

Webbe Tent, presented to Winchester College in memory of Herbert Webbe. A drawing by John Whittall from a contemporary sketch. *(D.J. Leighton)*

Hunter Tent. The new pavilion presented by the Hunter family to replace Webbe Tent in 1930. *(D.J. Leighton)*

Oak panelling at Winchester College bearing Montague's engraved name. *(D.J. Leighton)*

New College, Oxford. Montague studied here for four years. *(Andy Parlour)*

Above, left: Alexander Webbe, friend of Montague at Oxford and brother of Herbert. *(The Vaughan Library, Harrow School) Right:* Harold Christopherson, the oldest of the ten brothers, with Derman, the youngest, in 1881. Harold died the next year. *(D.J. Leighton)*

The Christopherson Brothers – the team that played against Blackheath in Montague's last cricket match. *(D.J. Leighton)*

KENNETH	DOUGLAS	MALCOLM	SIDNEY	PERCY
STANLEY	DERMAN (FATHER)	CECIL		
DERMAN (JUNIOR)	HORACE			

Above, left: Nicholas 'Felix'
Wanostrocht. A self-portrait
that hangs in Lord's pavilion.
(Marylebone Cricket Club)

Above, right: The 4th Lord
Harris, a formidable power in
English cricket for fifty years.
He was a team-mate and fellow
MCC committee member with
Montague. *(Marylebone Cricket
Club)*

Sir Francis Lacey, team-mate of
Montague. He served as MCC
Secretary, 1898–1926. This
picture hangs at Lord's.
(Marylebone Cricket Club)

9 Eliot Place
Blackheath
30th Decr 1885.

Sir

Your application for the post
of groundman to the Blackheath
Cricket, Football &c Company was
duly considered on Monday last
but I am sorry to inform you
it was not accepted.

Yours truly
M. I. Druitt
per A. P.

Mr G. Street
Kennington Oval

P. S.

Montague's letter to George Street. Nevertheless within a few weeks Street was appointed groundsman and remained so for thirty-eight years. *(Bert Street)*

The menu for the MCC Centenary Dinner. *(Marylebone Cricket Club)*

The Duke of Clarence surrounded by a group of his friends. Seven of the group were Apostles. Standing: J.N. Langley; top row, from left: A.H. Clough, J.K. Stephen, C.V. Stanford; seated, from left: H.B. Smith, J.N. Dalton, F.B. Winthrop, J.D. Duff, H.F. Wilson, J.W. Clark, HRH Duke of Clarence, H.C. Goodhart, H.L. Stephen, A.H. Smith. *(The Royal Archives)*

Below, left: The Duke of Clarence, 'ready for a night out'. *(D.J. Leighton) Right:* James Stephen. A painting by Charles Wellington Furse, which hangs in King's College, Cambridge. *(Provost and Fellows of King's College, Cambridge)*

Virginia Woolf as the wicket-keeper with her brother Adrian in the garden of Tallard House, St Ives. *(Tate Archive)*

9 King's Bench Walk. Montague's chambers were here. *(Andy Parlour)*

Thorneycroft Wharf, Chiswick, with The Osiers on the right. It was here that Montague was found drowned. *(The VT Group plc)*

Below, left: Montague's gravestone in Wimborne Cemetery. *(David McCleave) Right:* Sir Charles Warren, Metropolitan Police Commissioner, 1886–8, during whose tenure four of the five Ripper murders were committed. *(Historical Collection, Metropolitan Police)*

A contemporary sketch of the Kearley and Tonge head office, where the body of Catherine Eddowes was found. *(David McCleave)*

Entrance to the Cleveland Club. Note the immobile policeman. *(Illustrated Police News)*

THE HOUSE IN CLEVELAND ST: A DEN OF INFAMY.

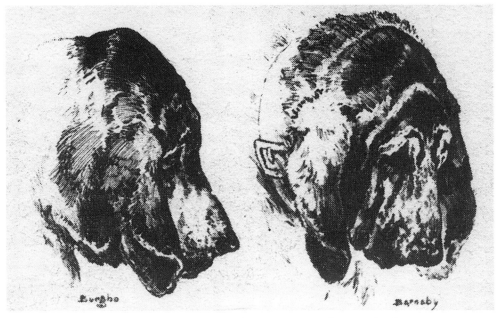

Burgho and Barnaby, bloodhounds tested by Charles Warren. *(Illustrated Police News)*

From The Evening News, Feb. 2nd, 1949.

Amelia Lewis, pictured as she tried to entice the Ripper. *(Evening News)*

Warren had been admitted to the Royal Arch of Masons in 1861, so he may have straightaway put his own interpretation on the message. Within hours of the murder he ordered it to be obliterated, despite the protests of the City Police. This was contrary to any sort of correct police procedure, and a clear legal offence. However, Warren was mindful of the Royal Arch of Masons' oath, which William Morgan in his book about freemasonry in 1836 describes thus: 'the oath taken by all Royal Arch Masons does not except murder and treason, therefore under it all crimes can be perpetrated.' So at that time a Royal Arch mason was compelled to cover up any crime of a fellow mason, even murder.

Catherine Eddowes is thought to have been killed in mistake for Mary Kelly, a misunderstanding that leads directly to the Duke of Clarence. He had become aware that Kelly knew about his illegitimate daughter by the Cleveland Street shop girl, Annie Crook, in 1885. She was, therefore, a serious threat. In 1888 the Duke was the Right Worshipful Master of the Alpha Lodge. Warren would therefore have seen it as his duty to protect a fellow mason, and he was in the ideal position to effect a cover-up. Six weeks later the real Mary Kelly was killed in a way horribly reminiscent of Jubela, Jubelum and Jubelo.

In the late ninteenth and early twentieth centuries, freemasonry ran through royalty, aristocracy, senior government, the police and the armed forces. The military earls Haig, Kitchener, Jellicoe and Alexander were all members. So were the 'civilian' dukes of Carnarvon, Derby, Limerick and, of particular interest, Euston. The Earl of Euston (Henry Fitzroy) was Lord Grafton's brother, and he often visited the Cleveland Street Club, sometimes known as 'Hammonds' after its owner. A male prostitute, John Saul, had known Charles Hammond for ten years. 'We both earned our living as Sodomites,' he told the police. He also gave the police this testimony: 'The young Duke of Grafton, I mean the brother of the present Duke, was a constant visitor at Hammonds . . . I saw him myself last night. I know him well.' This evidence was used in court when Lord Euston sued the editor of the *North London Press*, Ernest Parke, for libel. Parke had written criticising the disappearance abroad of Arthur Somerset and Charles Hammond before the Cleveland Street trial by claiming 'their prosecution would inculpate more highly placed and distinguished personages'. Lord Euston won his case when, perversely, Judge Henry Hawkins dismissed the evidence of Saul because he was a homosexual, and sent Parke to prison for a year. Someone had chosen the judge carefully. He had a reputation in civil cases for using various tricks and technicalities to avoid passing judgments. Henry Hawkins had performed as required.

It is unclear whether or not Sir William Gull was a mason, but he was certainly closely associated with men who were, such as Charles Warren and the Duke of Clarence. It was Gull who arranged sometime in 1886 for Annie Crook, the mother of the Duke of Clarence's child, to be moved from Cleveland Street and kept under observation in Guy's Hospital for five months. During this time he certified her insane. It is alleged Gull then performed an operation on her to cause memory loss, partial paralysis and reduced brain function. It was now safe, as far as the Duke of Clarence was concerned, for her to be released. For the next thirty years she led a thoroughly miserable life, drifting around hospitals and workhouses, deteriorating all the time. Finally, when completely insane, she was admitted on 20 February 1920 to the lunacy observation ward of St George's Union Infirmary in Fulham Road. Three days later she died.

There would have been few common denominators between the Apostles and the Freemasons. The members were very different in character, but one man who could have belonged to both clubs was Oscar Wilde. He unquestionably had the intellect, personality and the right friends to have joined the Apostles, but, like Montague, he was a graduate of Oxford not Cambridge, and therefore not eligible. However, he was a mason. A friend of Wilde's at Balliol College, Oxford, J.E.C. Bodley, interested him in the masonic costumes and rituals. Bodley recalls: 'Wilde was as much struck with their gorgeousness as he was amazed by the mystery of our conversation.' He was also taken by the knee breeches, tail coat, silk stockings and pumps. Wilde became a member of the Apollo Lodge on

23 February 1875. It was not a passing fad. Wilde, whose father had belonged to the Shakespeare Lodge in Dublin, enjoyed the masonic pomp and ceremonies, and rose to the rank of Master Mason within three months.

Although they had some mutual acquaintances and were at Oxford together, there is no evidence that Montague met Wilde, but he would certainly have been aware of him. Similarly he would have known of Wilde's friend, Lord Alfred Douglas, if only because both were Wykehamists. If Montague could have been a member of the Apostles or the Freemasons, it is more likely he would have chosen the former, as it would not have occurred to him to join the latter. He did not belong to the police or the military, and he had no governmental ambitions. Nor did he see freemasonry as a way of social or career advancement. There has been one suggestion that Montague's death owed something to freemasonry. The policeman who examined the body, George Moulson, recorded that he found four large stones in each pocket. These have been alternatively described as pieces of masonry, with the obvious association.

FOURTEEN

Mr Boultbee, at Your Service

There was one man who was privy to all the information, theories and secrets that passed across the desks of the men who served as Commissioner of the Metropolitan Police between 1886 and 1897. He was Walter Ernest Boultbee, and, extraordinarily, he was one of Montague's relations. Boultbee was married to Ellen Baker, who was a niece of Alfred Mayo. His cousin was Montague's grandmother Jane Mayo. This relationship was not close but it was real. Boultbee's position throughout this period was Private Secretary to the three Commissioners.

He took up his post in 1886 when he was asked to work for the newly appointed General Sir Charles Warren. All Warren's experience had been in the army, mostly serving in Griqualand West and fighting the Kaffir Wars. Suppressing native uprisings in the southern parts of Africa was his forte. In Egypt he gained a reputation for detective work among the Bedouin. This helped him achieve his position, although the experience gained abroad in a war-time situation was not really relevant to policing London in peace time. He was also a keen archaeologist, and in the earlier part of his life he had conducted surveys and excavations in Palestine. In retirement he wrote a highly learned tome entitled *The Early Weights and Measures of Mankind.*

Warren could perform many tasks admirably, but police work was not one of them. He knew only one style of leadership and that was harshly military. In 1887 he appointed five military officers to take control of demonstrations in London. These men, together with thousands of policemen and 600 Grenadier Soldiers and Life Guards, managed to break up and clear the protesting mass of the unemployed in Trafalgar Square, but it was an expensive success bought at the price of public alienation from the police.

The Home Secretary to whom Warren was responsible was Henry Matthews, and his Private Secretary was the omnipresent Evelyn Ruggles-Brise. Ruggles-Brise was Private Secretary to four Home Secretaries during the same period as Boultbee worked for the commissioners. This was the time when the Whitechapel murders were foremost in the minds of the authorities and the people of the East End. Warren was unbendingly certain of his own decisions, became bad-tempered when challenged and saw no need for tact. His relationship with the Home Secretary soon declined, and he resigned on 8 November 1888. It was the day before the fifth murder, but his stewardship had covered the previous four. His failure to discover and convict the murderer contributed to his resignation.

By all accounts Warren worked hard to catch the murderer, but the continuing failure of the police to achieve a result reflected personally on Warren. Unusually he was persuaded, partly by public demand and partly by the successful arrest of a murderer twelve years earlier in Blackburn, to experiment with bloodhounds to track the killer. Trials with two dogs, Barnaby and Burgho, took place in early October in Regent's Park and went quite well, although there was a setback when the animals were let loose on Tooting Common. To the delight of the onlookers, the dogs ran off. Nevertheless Warren ordered that, if there was another body, it should not be moved until the dogs came in. On 9 November, the day after Warren's resignation, Mary Kelly was found and proceedings were held up for the dogs to arrive. Unfortunately they had already been taken back to their home in Scarborough, as their owner Edwin Brough would not agree financial terms for their use with Scotland Yard. A tragedy was turning into a farce. The trials with the bloodhounds did provoke some ridicule, but it was Warren's unpopularity with the public and the police force, and his difficult relationship with Henry Matthews, that meant his Commissioner days were numbered.

Warren did try one other unconventional means of trapping the murderer. In the autumn of 1888, with Ripper fever at its height, he was persuaded by two detectives, Gill and Payne, to use a female decoy. This was as radical as it was dangerous, for at the time women were not allowed to enter the police force. The 20-year-old woman was called Amelia Lewis, and she was the daughter of a Stepney licensee. Armed only with a whistle, she walked round the site of the old London Hospital at midnight with Gill and Payne hiding nearby. Suddenly in the darkness a rope dropped over a wall. She blew her whistle and the detectives were there immediately. But to no avail. When her father heard of her escapade, she was forbidden to go out at night again. Amelia Lewis (or Mrs Brown as she became) always believed that 'Jack the Ripper was a doctor and he was after me that night'. At least she survived to tell the tale. She produced twelve children and lived into her eighties in Peckham. The plan was illustrated in the *London Evening News* on 2 February 1949 with drawings of Amelia as a young woman and as an old lady. To one side is an impression of an investigating sleuth looking very much like Sherlock Holmes.

It was Warren who had rubbed the 'Juwes' message off the wall after the fourth murder, but now another sort of writing was on the wall and he was on his way out. Walter Boultbee would have known everything about Warren's tenure, and could have assessed what, if anything, Warren achieved in his hunt for the Ripper. He would also have understood just why Warren wiped that message off the wall. Warren never recovered from this experience of the civilian world. He returned to the army, but even his military reputation was lost when he was held responsible for the massacre of British troops on 24 January 1900 at the Battle of Spion Kop during the Boer War.

He has been described as 'arguably the most incompetent British Commander of the whole Second Boer War of 1899–1902'. Later, his help in the relief of Ladysmith enabled him to be promoted to General and shortly before his retirement in 1906 he became Colonel Commandant of the Royal Engineers. At that time Edward, Montague's brother, was still serving in the Royal Engineers, having returned from Australia in 1893. In retirement Warren wrote his book about ancient weights and measures and joined his old friend Lord Baden Powell in establishing the Boy Scout movement. He even formed his own Boy Scout Troop known as the 1st Ramsgate or 'Sir Charles Warren's Own'. He had survived the trauma of four Ripper murders, and the shambles of Spion Kop to enjoy a full and varied life. When he died in 1927, aged 87, he left one strange legacy. It seems that the public always associated Warren with his monocle, to such an extent that a Harold Trevor always wore one and liked to be known as 'Sir Charles Warren'. Trevor was hanged in 1941 for murdering a prostitute.

There was some evidence in James Monro's background that he was suitable for senior police work. He had worked in the Indian Civil Service from 1857 as a magistrate and later as a Civil Sessions judge. Afterwards he became Inspector General of the Police in Bengal. In 1884 he returned to England on his appointment as Assistant Commissioner in charge of the CID. However, his rather autocratic, colonial style was a problem, and he argued frquently with the Commissioner, Charles Warren. Monro wished to appoint Melville Macnaghten as his Assistant Chief Constable, but Warren could not agree. Monro and Macnaghten had been friends since the early 1880s in India when Macnaghten had been assaulted by some natives.

The disagreement was symptomatic of the power struggle for control of the CID. Warren prevailed and James Monro resigned. However, Monro was not lost to the police service: he was instructed to set up a secret government detective organisation by the Home Secretary, Henry Matthews. Its task was to keep an eye on any group considered subversive such as anarchists and Irish Nationalists – it was a forerunner of today's Special Branch.

Two years later, when Warren resigned, it was, ironically, James Monro whom Matthews chose to replace him as the Commissioner of the Metropolitan Police.

Because of his interest in detective work, Monro became thoroughly immersed in the Ripper case, and when a further murder occurred that bore all the familiar hallmarks he was soon on the scene. The victim was Alice McKenzie, a prostitute, who died on 17 July 1889 in Castle Alley, Whitechapel. Her throat had been cut and her body mutilated. At the inquest Dr Thomas Bond stated clearly: 'I am of the opinion that the murder was performed by the same person who committed the former series of Whitechapel murders.' This was Monro's view as well. If the two men were right, then Montague is innocent. In retirement Monro said, 'The Ripper was never caught but he should have been,' and he hinted that the murderer could have been an establishment figure. His private view, he said, was 'a very hot potato'.

Despite his concern with matters in the East End, Monro's priority was to suppress Irish Nationalist factions in their quest for Home Rule. He ran a controversial espionage campaign into the activities of the Irish Members of Parliament in an attempt to connect them with the bombings in England. Although he was popular with rank-and-file policemen and with his staff, he could be individualistic and awkward with those senior to him. He was similar in character to Henry Matthews, to whom he reported at the Home Office. It was inevitable, therefore, that theirs was not a close relationship. Matthews, a Catholic, was most uneasy with Monro's methods of unearthing Irish Home Rule supporters. In June 1889 Monro got his way and appointed Melville Macnaghten Assistant Chief Constable. This act was to have unforeseen repercussions on Montague's reputation and brought Montague an undeserved notoriety.

Macnaghten never forgot his friendship with Monro. In his autobiography, *Days of My Years*, he wrote: 'I doubt whether any of the gentlemen who filled his position before or after his time gained more completely the affection and confidence of their officers.'

James Monro had also played a reluctant part in the cover-up of the Cleveland Street scandal. When the appearance of Lord Arthur

Somerset at the trial seemed certain, the Prince of Wales instructed his civil servant Sir Dighton Probyn to 'go and see Monro, go to the Treasury, see Lord Salisbury if necessary. Somerset's name must at all costs be cleared.' Prime Minister Salisbury managed to get the trial delayed to such an extent that Monro wrote to him in October saying: 'Proceedings in this case have been pending since the month of July, and I cannot but consider that it is unfair to the Metropolitan Police that the action should be, on account of this delay, exposed to the criticisms and mis-interpretation to which I have called your attention.' The trial soon began but not before Lord Somerset had disappeared.

Walter Boultbee witnessed all these conflicts of policy and personnel, and came close to working with Montague's old cricketing adversary, Evelyn Ruggles-Brise. Matthews wished to have Ruggles-Brise as an Assistant Chief Constable. As a long-time civil servant and administrator, Ruggles-Brise would have been entirely pliant to Matthews, but he had no military or police experience. This outraged Monro and he resigned. Ruggles-Brise did not get his promotion. Monro could have provided a large piece of the Whitechapel puzzle. Of all the senior policemen he was more informed about it than probably anyone else, and he was better placed to know the truth. However, he never published his memoirs, and only scraps of his opinions have been passed down.

Monro was not a member of the police force during the 1888 murders, but as head of the Detective Service he would have been consulted. He did, for example, visit the site of Mary Kelly's murder. His grandson James recalls him saying: 'it was terrible, even the ceiling was splashed with blood.' Furthermore, at the height of the furore Henry Matthews sent a memo to Ruggles-Brise: 'Stimulate the police about the Whitechapel murders. Monro might be willing to give a hint to the CID people if necessary.' After his resignation James Monro returned to Bengal and founded the Ranaghat Medical Mission, where he worked until 1905. He then returned to Scotland and died in 1920.

When James Monro resigned, the third commissioner for whom Walter Boultbee worked was appointed. He was Sir Edward Ridley

Colborne Bradford and he had what was generally considered a successful thirteen years in office. Sir Edward came from a familiar military background. He entered the Madras Cavalry in 1853 and served in the Persian Campaign in 1857. His first experience of police work came the following year when he was put in command of the 1st Central Indian Horse. This was, in effect, secret political work. Later on this developed into internal law and order control mostly relating to robberies and murders involving local tribes and sects. He was appointed Chief Commissioner in Ajmere, and then in 1887 came back to England to lead the Secret and Political Department at the India Office. His time in India had not been without its setback. In 1867 he had been enjoying a tiger hunt when the animal retaliated and destroyed his left arm. He managed to survive, and developed a technique of pig-sticking with one arm.

By all accounts his working style was friendly and tactful, and he managed to get his way by his own personal skills. He was not a dominating, high-profile leader in the mould of Charles Warren. Ruggles-Brise, as Private Secretary to Henry Matthews, records a disagreement Bradford had with the somewhat awkward Matthews. He wrote: 'If you couldn't get on with Bradford you could get on with nobody.' However, he was a secretive man by training, and much less forthcoming than he appeared. It was in 1892 under Bradford's period in charge that the file on the Ripper was officially closed, but there are no records of opinions he might have had on the subject. Whatever they were and however confidential, Walter Boultbee would have been aware of them. It is not known just how discreet Boultbee was or if he was used by any of the Commissioners as a conduit for information from the Druitt family; he could even have passed the latest police and Home Office thinking the other way. Whatever the truth, it is the oddest coincidence that a member of Montague's family was ever in such a position.

Sir Edward's policy towards the Whitechapel murders was apparently to leave matters to Macnaghten, now the Chief Constable. Nevertheless, during Sir Edward's tenancy there was one murder that is often referred to as a possible additional Ripper killing. This happened on 13 February 1891 when Frances Coles aged 26 and another prostitute had her throat slashed in Whitechapel. So the series of murders would have been a real issue to Sir Edward and one which he would not have been able to avoid entirely by delegation.

Sir Edward did fulfil one royal function that may have clinched his promotion to Commissioner. He had been detailed to accompany the Duke of Clarence on HMS *Oceana* when the Duke was discreetly removed from public view at the time of the Cleveland Street trial. Once in India, Sir Edward's role was to manoeuvre the Duke through the gamut of dinners, public functions, meetings with maharajahs and all the obligations of a full royal tour. The Duke, naturally, found time for traditional sporting activities such as pig-sticking, in which Sir Edward was now an expert. The tour began in October 1889 and ended in May 1890; within weeks Sir Edward got his appointment as Commissioner. When his time with the Metropolitan Police ended, he became Extra Equerry to Edward VII. The time he had spent with the King's elder son in India and on the *Oceana* may have been the most beneficial of his career.

Bradford and Boultbee were less than two years into their partnership when the New Year of 1892 began. It was to be an eventful year in respect of the Whitechapel killings and for the country as a whole. On 14 January it was announced that the second in line to the throne had died. The circumstances surrounding this statement were murky to say the least. The Duke's behaviour and his sexual deviances had aroused widespread concern, and his latest extravagance had been two attempts to burn down Sandringham House. As with so much in his life they were failures, but they confirmed the view of his increasingly worried parents and grandmother that as a monarch he would be a disaster. A month earlier he had become engaged to Princess May of Teck and already she was uneasy about the union. 'Can I really take this on?' she asked her mother. For a week before his death there were reports of influenza, and this illness was soon described as pneumonia. It was convenient indeed for the future of the monarchy when his doctors could pronounce to the nation that he was dead.

Even as the country mourned, the rumours began that the Duke was beginning a new life hidden away in Glamis Castle. Another story suggested he had been sent to Osborne House on the Isle of Wight. Anecdotal evidence to support these claims has been passed down from Dr Stowell who worked with Theodore Dyke Acland and who was a friend of Sir William Gull and his daughter Caroline. However, one way or another, the Duke was officially out of the way.

At the funeral at Windsor there was a small group of the Duke's Cambridge friends, all Apostles. They were Harry Wilson, Henry Goodhart and Harry Cust. The three had received an invitation for the choir area of St George's Chapel, an inner sanctum reserved only for the closest or most distinguished of the Duke's friends. Wilson wrote sadly of the occasion and mentioned James Stephen, who by now was certified insane. 'We were not without a thought for poor Jim Stephen, who would certainly have been with us if fate had not stricken him too, though in a different way. I need not say we were proud of the honour done us.'

Among the mourning tears, some real, some crocodile, the news to James Stephen was devastating. By 1892 Stephen's mental capacity was collapsing, and now he disintegrated with grief. He was already resident in St Andrew's Lunatic Asylum at Northampton, and now he refused all food. Twenty-one days later on 3 February he was dead. His death was attributed to 'mania, refusal of food, exhaustion'.

There was a strange element of instability that ran through the Stephen family. James's father, Sir James Fitzjames Stephen, the judge in the Maybrick trial, had to resign from the bench in 1891 because of a serious brain disorder. His uncle Leslie was prone to depressions and had three nervous breakdowns. James also had a cousin Laura and her feeble-mindedness was to end in madness. Another cousin, Thoby Stephen, tried to kill himself as a schoolboy. The writer Virginia Woolf, who was the sister of Laura and Thoby and therefore also a cousin of James, became a Woolf by her marriage to Leonard. Leonard considered suicide when Britain was under threat in 1940.

As an impressionable child Virginia Woolf would have listened to her uncle and cousin James relate the Ripper story in which they were both involved. She would have been told the circumstances and manner of Montague's death. It is clear these details remained with her for the rest of her life. She, too, suffered depression and mental illness. Finally in 1941 she eerily chose to copy the way Montague died, as it had been told to her. On 28 March she wrote a note to her husband: 'I know I shall never get over this (madness) and I am wasting your life.' Virginia left Monk's House, her home at Rodmell just south of Lewes in Sussex, and walked to the river Ouse, wearing a winter coat with deep pockets. She filled these pockets with heavy stones and waded into the river. Her body, like Montague's, was not discovered for four weeks, and the coroner's verdict was the same.

Walter Boultbee would have been privy to all the comings and goings of 1892, but there is nothing in his background to suggest he was anything but discreet. He was born in 1853, joined the Civil Service from Leeds Grammar School and married Ellen Baker in 1885. They had three children Walter, Thomas and Alice. In some ways Boultbee's career in the Civil Service mirrored that of Evelyn Ruggles-Brise at the Home Office. Sadly, however, the prospects of even more senior jobs and a knighthood were cut short when in late 1897 he caught pneumonia and died on 6 December of a heart attack. There was nothing suspicious about his early death. His wife and brother Hugh were with him at his home in Hampstead. His assets of £1,200 were modest.

With Boultbee's death was lost the opportunity for some important memoirs which would have given an invaluable insight into the remarkable events in the Metropolitan Police between 1886 and 1897. They could have revealed whether the Druitt family were ever asked for information about Montague, or indeed volunteered it. They could have shown whether Montague's name ever entered police discussions at all, and they could have supplied more of the real thoughts and conclusions of the three Commissioners, in respect of the murders. Walter Boultbee's story could have been the most important of all.

FIFTEEN

My Uncle Knew Ranjitsinhji

When Melville Macnaghten, an old Etonian, retired from the police in June 1913, he said in an interview for the *Morning Post*: 'I have two great regrets in my life – one is I was not allowed to play in the match against Harrow having been turned out of the eleven before the match, and the other that I joined the CID six months after the Whitechapel murderer committed suicide and I never had a go at him.'

Macnaghten worked at Scotland Yard because his old friend James Monro managed to secure him the position of Assistant Chief Constable in 1889. Macnaghten scarcely deserved the post. After he left Eton he went to India to manage the family estates in Bengal, taking over their administration from his uncle Chester, who had been asked by the Chiefs of Kathiawar to run Rajkumar College. This was a school established in 1870 for Indian princes, and most notable among its pupils was Prince Kumar Ranjitsinhji, who proved to be one of the finest batsmen of all time. He was the first Indian to play Test cricket, albeit for England. He recalled of the College: 'we had masters who were specially engaged to teach us cricket.' The *Lillywhite's Annual* for 1897 confirms this: 'At Rajkumar College the foundation of his cricket was laid by an Englishman.' That Englishman was Chester Macnaghten. Chester remained at Rajkumar College for twenty-five years, and was key to Ranjitsinhji's education on and off the cricket field. On the death of his father he inherited the title Maharaja Jam Sahib of Navanagar.

Despite his lack of appropriate policing experience, Macnaghten did the job well enough to be promoted to Chief Constable and to remain in the post until 1903. After that he continued in a variety of other police roles until his retirement ten years later. His fixation with the Ripper affair is slightly curious. For example, locked in his office desk he kept horrific mortuary photographs of the Ripper's victims, and in 1891 he inspected the body of Frances Coles at the murder site. Macnaghten arrived at Scotland Yard, as he says, six months after the fifth murder, and then as Chief Constable declared the case closed in 1892. He never explained why it was appropriate to make this decision. It is tempting to relate it to the deaths a few months earlier of the Duke of Clarence and James Stephen.

However, in his autobiography published in 1914 he claimed that the murderer committed suicide on or about 10 November 1888. Although this is three weeks before Montague's death, his remarks could be taken as a hint. Later he told his grandson that 'he believed the murderer to be a sex maniac who committed suicide after the (9 November) murder, possibly the young doctor whose body was found in the Thames on December 31 1888.' Without naming Montague, this takes the hint a stage further. Yet in his *Daily Mail* interview in 1913 he went on to say: 'Of course he [the murderer] was a maniac, but I have a clear idea who he was and how he committed suicide but that with other secrets will never be revealed by me. I have destroyed all my documents and there is now no record of the secret information which came into my possession at one time or another.' Even with a quarter of a century of hindsight he was reluctant to express any real opinion, much less name a suspect.

It is Macnaghten's handwritten notes, signed and dated 23 February 1894 but not found until the 1950s, that are the reason why the finger was ever pointed at Montague. There are two versions. One is held at Scotland Yard. It names Macnaghten's three main suspects:

> no one ever saw the Whitechapel murderer; many homicidal maniacs were suspected but no shadow of proof could be thrown on any one. I may mention the cases of three men, any one of whom would have been more likely than Cutbush (another suspect) to have committed this series of murders.
>
> 1. A Mr M.J. Druitt said to be a doctor, of good family, who disappeared at the time of the Miller's Court murder and whose body (which was said to have been upwards of a month in the water) was found in the Thames on 31 Dec – or about 7 weeks after the murder. He was sexually insane and from private info. I have, I have little doubt that his own family believed him to have been the murderer.

Macnaghten's two other suspects were a Polish Jew, Aaron Kosminski, and Michael Ostrog, a Russian doctor.

The second version, which was passed down by Lady Aberconway, Macnaghten's daughter, is similar but adds:

> Personally after much careful and deliberate consideration I am inclined to exonerate the last 2 but I have always held strong opinions regarding number one, and the more I think the matter over the stronger do these opinions become. The truth therefore will never be known and did indeed at one time lie at the bottom of the Thames, if my conjections [*sic*] be correct.

The Aberconway notes described Montague as 'a doctor of about 41 years of age and of fairly good family'.

It may seem strange that Macnaghten ever found the opportunity or the motivation to write these notes. It seems he had been provoked into action by a claim in the *Sun* newspaper on 13 February 1894 that it had solved the murders. Cutbush was not named, but it was generally realised that he was the *Sun*'s choice. The idea that a newspaper could solve such a crime goaded

Macnaghten into attacking their 'proof' through his notes, which he wrote ten days later. The case itself had been closed for two years, and he should have been immersed in his on-going Chief Constable duties. Yet he found time to put together a rambling thesis of nearly 2,000 words. It was as if he was writing his memoirs nearly twenty years before his retirement. In another age he might have been charged with wasting police time. The notes themselves are flawed. Montague was not a doctor, and did not disappear 'at the time of the Miller's Court [9 November] murder'. He attended a Blackheath Club board meeting on 19 November, and was at Valentine's school up to the date of his dismissal, which was 30 November. Nor was he 41 years of age, but 31.

The term 'sexually insane' is open to interpretation. Macnaghten probably intended it as a euphemism for homosexuality, perhaps based on a guess at the reason for Montague's dismissal. It could also be taken literally. Fifteen per cent of the male population in Victorian England had syphilis, and over the years it has affected all classes of society. Adolf Hitler was driven mad by it, and, according to the American historian Deborah Hayden in *Pox, Genius, Madness and the Mysteries of Syphilis*, Abraham Lincoln, Beethoven, Henry VIII and Ivan the Terrible were all sufferers. Recent BBC research quoted by the cricket writer Roger Heavens finds that John Wisden of Almanac fame was also a victim. He died prematurely in 1884.

Lord Randolph Churchill, sometime Chancellor of the Exchequer, father of Winston and Ripper suspect, caught syphilis, possibly from a Blenheim housemaid, and died from it in 1895 aged 46. He was a political ally of Lord Salisbury and a close friend of the royal family. When the Duke of Clarence collected his honorary degree at Cambridge in June 1888 he dined with Churchill. By now the disease had taken an irreversible grip, and he would have been happy to serve the Duke in any way he could in the time left to him. The historian A.J.P. Taylor said of Churchill: 'He might have been a great (Tory) leader. In retrospect he appears a great nuisance.' The Duke of Clarence may not have had syphilis, but he did have gonorrhoea, as the notes of his doctors show. This was a most dangerous disease. A German doctor Wilhelm Erb conducted a survey in the late 1800s and found that half of all male patients in lunatic asylums had gonorrhoea (a piece of research that perhaps only a nineteenth-century German doctor would have chosen to carry out).

Macnaghten may also have compiled his notes because he was under instructions to rewrite history. The controversy about the murders had not stopped with the closure of the case, and the notes were an attempt to consolidate a cover-up by implicating a man who was conveniently dead.

Macnaghten was in a better position than any of his contemporaries to claim access to Montague's family. Evidence of the closeness of the Macnaghten and Druitt families is found in C.H. Mayo's book *A Genealogical Account of the Mayo and Elton families* (1908). It states that John Mayo, brother of Montague's grandmother, 'for many years held an appointment in the East India House which he obtained through his friends the Melvills'. James Melvill was Secretary and Philip Melvill was Assistant Military Secretary of the East India Company. This was around 1830, and the name Melvill is significant. During the next generation Montague's uncle James Druitt married the same John Mayo's daughter, Matilda Jane, and they had a son called Melvill. He was named after the Melvills, who were godparents. Then in February 1855 Matilda Jane's brother, John Horsley Mayo, was appointed Writer in the East India House by the Chairman Elliot Macnaghten. He was Melville's father, and his father before him, Sir William Macnaghten, had also worked for the East India Company. John Horsley Mayo remained in touch with the Druitts and even visited Archdeacon Thomas Druitt (Montague's uncle) in Australia. Clearly, there had been a record of friendship and patronage between the Melvills, the Macnaghtens and the Mayos (and hence the Druitts) going back to the beginning of the century. So, if Melville Macnaghten wished for private family information and theories, he was well placed. Equally, he could attribute theories of his own to the family, and be given credibility because of his connections and position.

Another possible source connecting Macnaghten with information from Montague's family was a letter received by Sir Robert Anderson. Anderson was an Assistant Commissioner for the Metropolitan Police and was in charge of the Whitechapel Murder Investigation throughout the inquiry in 1888–92. An undated letter reached him sometime during that period from the 26th Earl of Crawford from his home at 2 Cavendish Square. It read:

My dear Anderson,

I send you this line to ask you to see and hear the bearer, whose name is unknown to me. She has or thinks she has a knowledge of the author of the Whitechapel murders. The author is supposed to be nearly related to her, and she is in great fear lest any suspicions attach to her and place her and her family in peril.

Very sincerely yours,

Crawford

The 26th Earl was James Ludovic Lindsay of Eton and Trinity College, Cambridge. There was a connection between the Lindsays and the Druitts. Emily Druitt, Montague's cousin, worked on six books of poetry by William Blake. The nickname and symbol she liked to use was 'owl', and when she was 18 she had written a long poem called 'The Owl and the Admiral'. This she sent to someone called Rear Admiral K. Fitzroy. It clearly referred to the two of them. So later on it was not surprising Emily developed a professional interest in poetry, and one of her William Blake books was published by Quaritch. Quaritch, who was also a book dealer, had a long-standing relationship with the Lindsay family, and was the Lindsays' main source of rare books for the Bibliotheca Lindesiana. James Lindsay continued this friendly relationship.

By a process of logic, theory and guesswork, it is possible to put forward a scenario in which Emily passed her suspicions to Quaritch, who told James Lindsay. Lindsay then agreed to introduce Emily to Anderson. Hence the letter of introduction. If the meeting had yielded anything significant, it could have been passed on to

Macnaghten and formed the basis of his 'private information'. However, he would surely have acted on it at the time or related it in his memoirs. If Anderson had been convinced by the woman's story, it is more likely to have implicated the Polish Jew Kosminski, not Montague, since Kosminski was Anderson's first choice in his autobiography. Kosminski was, of course, one of Macnaghten's three main suspects.

It is not surprising that the Earl of Crawford was approached to secure an interview for the woman with Robert Anderson. He was known to take an interest in the murders and wrote an article in December 1888 in the *Pall Mall Gazette*: 'In endeavouring to sift a mystery like this, one cannot afford to throw aside any theory, however extravagant, because the truth might, after all, lie in the most unlikely one.'

Emily's 'Owl and the Admiral' poem provides such a theory. The name Fitzroy gives the possibility of a link with the Duke of Grafton's family. This would lead to Lord Euston (Henry James Fitzroy) and Lord Somerset, both of whom were heavily implicated in the Cleveland Street affair. The Admiralty library has no record of a naval officer named 'K. Fitzroy' in the nineteenth century. However, it was appropriate to give the name Fitzroy a senior naval rank, as the name was strongly associated with that of Admiral Robert Fitzroy at the time, a major seafaring figure in the mid-nineteenth century and the grandson of the 3rd Duke of Grafton. The only K. Fitzroy of that period connected with this family was Katherine Fitzroy, the second daughter of Admiral Robert. She would have been about four years older than Emily when the poem was written. If the poem was to Katherine, the rank given to her was just a mild teenager's joke between friends, a reference to her father.

Lord Euston was the eldest son of a later Duke of Grafton. The Graftons, Eustons and Fitzroys were all part of the same family. This would make another connection between the Druitt family, the Cleveland Street affair and the Whitechapel murders. According to Walter Sickert, Somerset and Euston were in the East End on the nights of the murders acting as lookouts while their friends were at work.

Macnaghten's autobiography is no more reliable than his 1894 notes when it comes to implicating Montague. In addition to the factual errors already described, he writes: 'I incline to the belief that the individual who held up London in terror resides with his own people; that he absented himself from home at certain times.' Neither opinion applies to Montague, who had left home eight years earlier and had been based continuously ever since at 9 Eliot Place, Blackheath. His main reasons for occasional visits to Wimborne were to play cricket, and to carry out legal work in the area.

Of all the policemen involved in the Ripper case, Macnaghten had the widest range of contacts. Only he had social access to a more liberal society. He knew Oscar Wilde, Walter Sickert, James Whistler, Frank Miles, James Stephen and a range of actors, actresses and writers on a personal level. He lived in a fashionable street in Chelsea close to several of them, and in all probability dined and socialised with them. Here he would have picked up the latest gossip. All this would have improved the quantity if not the quality of his information, and could have provided a temptation to expound dubious theories.

Macnaghten claimed in his autobiography that 'The Whitechapel murderer committed five murders and – to give the devil his due – no more'. The fifth was Mary Kelly. This may have been a convenient conclusion to improve his case against Montague, yet Macnaghten could have unwittingly strengthened the cover-up or conspiracy theory. The murders stopped because Mary Kelly, who knew all about the Duke of Clarence's secret child, was dead. The object had been achieved.

One of the purposes of the notes was to shift blame from Thomas Cutbush. It so happened that Cutbush was a nephew of a senior Scotland Yard detective, Superintendent Charles Henry Cutbush, who shot himself in 1896 'because he knew nephew Thomas was the murderer'. Macnaghten's notes were his exoneration of a police colleague and his family, and a response to the preposterous suggestion that a newspaper could solve a crime that had defeated London's finest. If the *Sun* had not published its article, Macnaghten would not have written his document containing its unsubstantiated references to private family information about Montague. If that had been the case, there would never have been a suggestion that Montague had anything to do with the affair at all, and his name would never have been mentioned.

The mystery about Macnaghten has not been his notes, but why he should have continued to spend so much time and effort on a case that he himself had declared closed two years earlier. With the help of this double explanation, the reasons are clear and they do not show Macnaghten's integrity or professionalism in a good light.

SIXTEEN

The Judgment of Solomons

Only one living man was ever accused of being Jack the Ripper, and that man was Sir Arthur Conan Doyle. It happened more than twenty years after the murders when Doyle was on a tour of Australia promoting spiritualism. In Sydney, a woman incensed by what she considered witchcraft shouted out that he was Jack the Ripper. The Whitechapel murders had always been of great interest in Australia, especially since the bogus confessions of Frederick Deeming.

The woman's outburst was not entirely unreasonable, for Doyle's background and behaviour through the crucial years provided a better basis for suspicion than some of the more popular suspects. Nearly all the doctors, coroners and police surgeons who worked on the murders believed the killer had some medical training, and Doyle was more than qualified in this respect. When he was 17 he entered Edinburgh University as a medical student, and took several part-time doctoring jobs. His first full-time job was working as a surgeon on a Greenland whaling ship during a seven-month tour of the Arctic. It was during this time that Doyle showed a sadistic enjoyment for killing. The whaling ship also culled seals, and 'the moment the season began Doyle was on the ice helping to kill the older seals with a rifle and clubbing the skulls of the young ones.' In Doyle's words, the work 'showed what a man is made of', and he described the sound of the terrified seals as 'a noise between the mew of a cat and the bleat of a lamb'. His personal tally was fifty-five seals. His enthusiasm for killing whales was no less. There was also a sinister undertone when he qualified as a doctor the following year, and drew a self-portrait of a dancing figure waving a diploma. The caption read 'licensed to kill'.

After a further expedition, this time as a ship's doctor on a steamer bound for West Africa, he returned and in 1882 set up as a general practitioner in Southsea, where he remained for nine years. He was therefore within a reasonble distance of London for the crucial years and was medically qualified to inflict the murderous damage on the women.

Physically he was a powerful man. His height was 6ft 2in, he weighed 16 stone and he took body-building courses to improve his strength and appearance. Nor could he be termed a gentle giant. As a strapping teenager he beat up a youth in a tough slum area in his home town of Edinburgh, and soon after arriving in Southsea he laid out a sailor in an argument over a woman. A few years later, still in the Portsmouth area, he attacked some hecklers who were shouting abuse at a political meeting at which Arthur Balfour was speaking. On another occasion he struck his youngest son Adrian when he made a disparaging remark about a woman. Violence was a part of Doyle's character. He also promoted boxing tournaments, and was even invited to referee the world heavyweight boxing title fight in 1910 between James Jeffries and Jack Johnson in Nevada. Reluctantly he had to turn down the offer. He once remarked in a letter to G.K. Chesterton that he would rather have been a boxer than a writer.

Partly because of his physique Doyle was a good all-round sportsman. As well as playing very good standard cricket with the MCC and the Incogniti, he also, while living in Southsea, captained Portsmouth Cricket Club. He later played many matches for

Norwood, Grayshott and for the wandering side, the Allahakberries, run by J.M. Barrie, the creator of Peter Pan. He was a founder member of Portsmouth Football Club, and served on the British Olympic Association Committee that organised the 1908 London Olympiad. These activities gave him a rich range of social connections especially within cricket. Out of 3,000 MCC members only 100 were invited to a celebration lunch to welcome back the successful MCC side from Australia in 1912. Doyle was on the guest list, which included some old friends and acquaintances of Montague such as Lord Harris, Francis Lacey, John Shuter, Alexander Webbe and Ivo Bligh. He was clearly a man honoured at the highest level in a number of different social circles.

It is, however, his involvement with the Ripper murders that is somewhat suspicious. In 1888, as an emerging crime writer, he was asked to give his views on how to catch the killer. His ideas were strangely fanciful to the point of perhaps being deliberately misleading. He suggested that the murderer had disguised himself as a midwife or abortionist to explain the bloodied clothes. Later an American journalist asked for his views and Doyle said he recognised some American style and spelling in the Ripper's 'Dear Boss' letter, and suggested that the handwriting should be advertised in leading newspapers in the States in the hope that a member of the public might recognise it. This was done but proved to be useless. The real reason for this suggestion may have been more self-interested: Doyle was keen to promote himself and the Sherlock Holmes stories, which he had begun in 1887, in the USA. This strategy proved most successful, and he was asked to undertake lecture tours. His reputation, synonymous with that of Sherlock Holmes, became huge in America. This fame has endured. When items from Doyle's private archive came up for auction in London in May 2004, a preview of the main items was held in New York.

Doyle's promotion of the Jack the Ripper story in the United States had one unlikely result. In the late 1930s the American abstract artist Jackson Pollock was developing a new technique by which the paint was dripped onto the canvas. He became known as 'Jack the Dripper'. It was because of his friendship with

President Theodore Roosevelt and the demands of the American market that Doyle was persuaded in 1902 to resurrect Sherlock Holmes after his 'death' at the Reichenbach Falls. *The Hound of the Baskervilles* was the outcome.

As reported in the *Ripperologist* magazine, there are still Sherlock Holmes appreciation societies in the United States; one of them is the Abbey Grangers, led by Tom Smith. He explained Holmes's immediate popularity in England.

> Doyle, by luck, had created a detective who had greater brains than London's Metropolitan Police . . . The public wanted desperately to believe a person was out there able to solve crimes. Readers naturally relished Holmes' low opinion of both law enforcement groups and smiled over the ease with which he topped their best men who simply lacked any creativity or thought.

Holmes's low opinion of the police was a reflection of how Doyle felt. If anyone benefited from the murders it was Doyle. It is known that he went on an organised tour of the murder sites in the East End, and inspected police records, including the Ripper letters in Scotland Yard's Black Museum. On 4 July 1894 in the *Portsmouth Evening News* Doyle gave his view on the letter dated 25 September 1888: 'I remember going to the Scotland Yard museum and looking at the letter which was received by the police and which purported to come from the Ripper. Of course it may have been a hoax, but there were reasons to think it was genuine.' His interest seemed to go beyond casual curiosity or a vehicle for self-promotion. It was Doyle's stated view that all prostitutes were 'vile women', and he deplored the closure of museums during the First World War when the brothels stayed open. He also believed that the fact that at least 20 per cent of the army had venereal disease was exclusively the fault of these women.

Doyle had a staunchly Catholic education at Stonyhurst College and, although he had lost his faith, it was surprising that even as a lapsed Catholic he should become a Freemason. In July 1887 he joined the masons' Portsmouth branch called the Phoenix Lodge

No. 257. To do this he risked excommunication, but perhaps he felt the social and professional benefits were worth this chance. One of Doyle's new colleagues in freemasonry was Oscar Wilde, and, despite being so dissimilar, the two became friends. Doyle was the professional storyteller, a doctor and surgeon, smart and direct; Wilde was the languid bohemian who delighted in all things fey and artistic for their own sake. Doyle described a meeting with Wilde: 'it was indeed a golden evening for me.' Wilde in turn expressed his admiration, rather surprisingly, for Doyle's early work *Micah Clarke*. This was a historical novel and indicated Doyle's admiration for the austerity of the Puritans. Wilde was self-critical in his praise of Doyle: 'My work lacks those two great qualities that your work possesses – sincerity and strength. I throw probability out of the window for the sake of a phrase, and the chance of an epigram makes me desert truth.'

Once his writing became established Doyle built up a formidable list of social contacts. He was a close friend of Arthur Balfour, liked the young Winston Churchill and dined regularly with Edward VII. Within months of ascending to the throne, Edward knighted Doyle, apparently for writing a gritty defence of the government's policies in South Africa.

From his letters it is clear that the Ripper had a contempt of the police. He wrote: 'there is never a policeman near when I am at work' and 'what fools the police are. I even given them the name of the street where I am living.' Doyle for his part was equally dismissive: 'Oddly enough, the police did not, as far as I know, think of that,' he wrote. Later he described the detectives involved on the case as 'a bad bunch'. Doyle's involvement in the solution of the Whitechapel crimes was unhelpful, even misleading, yet on at least two occasions he showed that his literary skills could be applied in the real world of crime detection. He took up the case of a George Edalji who had been wrongly imprisoned and helped to clear his name. Even more famously, his contribution, including a booklet, assisted in the release of Oscar Slater. This was after Slater had been convicted of a murder in Scotland. It seems that, if it suited him, Doyle could be helpful to the course of justice.

Doyle even admitted that he had gained inspiration from the crimes, and wrote a story called 'Jack the Harlot Killer' which portrayed a policeman as the murderer. There has always been an association between Doyle and the Ripper, sometimes through the character of Sherlock Holmes. In recent times there have been at least two films featuring Holmes trying to track down the murderer. One was *Murder by Decree* in 1979 and the other *A Study in Terror* in 1973.

The police never forgot Doyle's interest in real-life mysteries, and nearly forty years after Whitechapel, at the age of 67, he was asked to help find the missing Agatha Christie. Using his knowledge of psychic science in which he was now an acknowledged expert, he predicted she would be found 'next Wednesday'. In fact she was discovered at a health spa the day before, but Doyle's assessment was better than that of the police, who believed she was dead. Still showing an eagerness for self-promotion, Doyle claimed his prediction a triumph for psychometry.

There is, of course, no direct evidence that Doyle had any untoward involvement in the Whitechapel murders, but this is true of all the people who have been held to be suspect. The possibility of their guilt is no stronger than Doyle's. He was a qualified surgeon, lived within distance of Whitechapel for the whole period, was prone to violence, and at the time of the murders was a strong 29-year-old. Recent research has shown that those found guilty of brutal or sexual attacks on women have often been, like Doyle, keen body-builders. He had the incentive and opportunity to mislead the police by directing them towards America for the benefit of his own career and possibly his own safety. Furthermore, he had a documented hatred of prostitutes and showed an inordinate interest in the murders by doing a tour of the sites, visiting the Black Museum and incorporating elements of the killings into a story. Also, by joining the Freemasons (a most unusual move for a Catholic), he had secured a protective web, and he shared with the Ripper a contempt for contemporary policemen and their methods.

To this day a strange and unexplained rumour surrounds Doyle's name: it is known as the 'Curse of Conan Doyle'. Both his sons died young and his papers have been subject to lengthy legal arguments. Most recently a Sherlock Holmes expert, Richard Lancelyn Green, died by garrotte aged 50 while disputing ownership of some private papers. An open verdict was passed. As one expert put it, 'the family has more of a curse on them than Tutankhamen'. The reason for this 'curse' is unknown, but it adds to the general view that Doyle was an enigma who had facets of his life that remain unrevealed.

A more famous boxing promoter, this time from the 1950s, Jack Solomons, used to say that, if a challenger had to withdraw from a title bout, it was essential to replace him with a better contender. If Montague's name falls from the lists, as it should, who better to replace him than Arthur Conan Doyle. At least one member of MCC and the Incogniti would be replaced by another.

SEVENTEEN

Joining up the Dots

There is a great deal of circumstantial evidence to suggest that Montague had nothing to do with the murders, and there remains no direct evidence against him.

It is known that he was playing cricket on days extremely close to the dates of the first two murders. The first murder was on 31 August, and he played in Wimborne the following day. The second was actually on the same day that he appeared for Blackheath. Theoretically it was just possible to combine the murders with the cricket, but it is most improbable.

For the last three murders he had an extremely sound alibi: he was working. Stawell Heard, the Blackheath historian, shares the view of Neil Rhind, a past chairman of the Blackheath Society, that Montague was the night-duty master at George Valentine's school. Montague had limited teaching responsibilities: his role was to take charge of the boys at night and carry out some sports coaching. Therefore Montague was either asleep, or awake on duty. Either way there were some forty pupils who could testify to his presence. The Michaelmas term would have begun in mid-September, in time to cover the last three killings.

On 29 October 1888 a letter was sent to Dr Thomas Openshaw, the curator at the London Hospital, Whitechapel, which enclosed a piece of human kidney. The sender claimed he had cut it from Catherine Eddowes. The kidney matched the remains of the dead woman's body. The police believed that the letter and its contents had come from the murderer. In 2002 Patricia Cornwell, the American crime writer, tracked down a letter sent in 1876 from Oxford by Montague to his uncle, and she commissioned a DNA comparison between the two letters. It was the first time DNA had been used in this case. The two readings had nothing in common, and Ms Cornwell concludes that Montague could not have written the 'Openshaw' letter. She goes on to say in the context of the DNA test: 'I do not believe that Druitt had a thing to do with murder and mutilation.' The very latest twenty-first-century technology therefore clears Montague of at least the Eddowes murder. If the belief that the five murders were committed by the same person is correct, this evidence clears him completely.

Pamela Ball in *Jack the Ripper: A Psychic Investigation* analyses all the leading suspects using her specialist knowledge of astrology and the psyche. It is an assessment from a different perspective from anything attempted previously. Several of her conclusions about Montague's character fit with what we already know of his life. For example, 'he could be extremely reasonable, adopting a rational and fair minded approach to whatever issue was at hand' and 'family solidarity and responsibility would have been important to him' and finally 'he loved all the grandeur and energy and the flamboyant display of big emotions'. It would have bored Montague to sit around and theorise too long. Ms Ball does not believe that Montague's dismissal was related to child molesting, and concludes that 'his astrological profile showed an inability to murder'.

An analysis of the letter that Montague sent to George Street in December 1885 supports Ms Ball's opinions. Elaine Quigley, one of Britain's leading graphologists and a past Chairman of the British Institute of Graphologists, examined the letter with no prior knowledge of Montague. Her conclusions were that he was a reliable, well-educated, confident person, who handled people well and was socially adept. She believed he would have been enthusiastic and efficient at any task confronting him and would have shown loyalty in a family or team situation. He was someone who liked to get on with a job, but not in an overbearing way. Furthermore he was probably kind, friendly and emotionally stable. Mrs Quigley could see no sign that he was capable of murder, much less a premeditated act, nor that he was violent or devious. There were no signs of latent homosexuality, and she regarded as most unlikely that he had any inclination to suicide. It is significant that the Street letter was written less than three years before Montague died. The readings are therefore strongly indicative of his true character.

Nearly all the coroners and doctors believed, and said so in their reports, that the murderer had at least some medical knowledge. Montague had none. He was classicist, schoolmaster and barrister.

It was often said that Montague's mental health had declined once his mother had been admitted to an asylum in July 1888 and that he was on the edge of breakdown. It is also pointed out that there was a history of instability in the family. The real evidence is that neither affected Montague. When his mother was sent to Clapton hospital, Montague showed no signs of being unduly upset. He did not move close to her. On the contrary, he spent half of July and the whole of August playing cricket in the Bournemouth area, and only came back to Blackheath to play in the club match and prepare for the new term. We know he was completely coherent and sensible at a board meeting of the Blackheath Club on 19 November. The idea that he inherited a family mental trait is also a fallacy, as the problem affected only the female members. His grandmother, aunt, mother and later his sister certainly did have mental problems, but none of the male members suffered. His three brothers, William, Edward and Arthur, all had good careers with no suggestion of difficulties. His grandfather and father were cornerstones of the medical profession and society in Wimborne, so if there was a family genetic weakness it did not affect the men.

The six most senior police officers who were involved in the case (Charles Warren, Melville Macnaghten, Frederick Abberline, James Monro, Edward Bradford, Robert Anderson) never formed a collective view of the murders, although the first three all thought the Ripper was a doctor of medicine. Macnaghten, as we know, chose Montague, Kosminski and Ostrog; Anderson also plumped for Kosminski, and Abberline selected Severin Klosowski, who was also known as George Chapman.

Frederick Abberline was another senior policeman who was very well informed about the case. He was in charge of a team of detectives in the East End and became Chief Inspector at Scotland Yard in 1890. His knowledge of the East End was excellent, but his opinions were variable. At one point he told a journalist that the murderer was a long way up the London social ladder. Yet when Klosowski was arrested (in 1902) for other murders, Abberline is alleged to have said to the arresting officer George Godley: 'You've got Jack the Ripper at last.' He then wrote to Melville Macnaghten with his theories. Yet within a few weeks he had changed his mind and admitted defeat. 'No; the identity of the diabolical individual has yet to be established, notwithstanding the people who have produced these rumours.' The same year Abberline went further and actually exonerated Montague. 'Yes I know about the story. But what does it amount to? Simply this. Soon after the last murder in Whitechapel, the body of a young doctor was found in the Thames, but there is absolutely nothing beyond the fact that he was found at the time to incriminate him.' By 'a young doctor' Abberline was undoubtedly referring to Montague. Warren, Monro and Bradford made no selections. It is noticeable that, where opinions were expressed, the accusations were made against people ill able to defend themselves, and with no risk of retribution. Montague was dead and Klosowski and Kosminski were impoverished Eastern European immigrants.

Either at the time or since a rich list of eminently famous suspects could be compiled covering royalty, the arts, literature, medicine, politics and the Law. Naming but one in each category, this would be, in order, the Duke of Clarence, Walter Sickert,

Charles Dodgson (Lewis Carroll), Sir William Gull, Randolph Churchill and James Stephen. Suspicion hovered over two or three of these characters at the time, but the Establishment ensured it remained unfocussed.

Frederick Abberline looks to have been party to this sort of cover-up. His diaries show that he was suspicious of James Stephen, Lord Randolph Churchill and Sir William Gull. He interviewed the three and then sent a note to the Chancellor of the Exchequer George Goschen (the same George Goschen who was a guest of honour at the MCC Centenary Dinner). Goschen had nothing to do with the Whitechapel enquiry, but was a close friend of Lord Randolph. It will also be recalled that earlier in 1889 the Prince of Wales had told his Civil Servant Sir Dighton Probyn 'to go to the Treasury' to suppress Lord Somerset's name in connection with the Cleveland Club trial. So Goschen as Chancellor could have become involved in the whole business of establishment cover-ups with a brief to look after the financial implications. The letter from Frederick Abberline to Goschen dated 15 December 1889 read:

Sir,
    With respect to your last instruction my interviews with J.K. Stephen, Lord Randolph Churchill, and Sir W. Gull were confirmed. I am sending this report for your personal attention. No further investigation will be made. I leave this in your hand. I have done my duty. Rest of my report will be sent on.
    Yours respectfully
    DI [Detective Inspector] F.G. Abberline

The reason for this private note is not hard to find. Abberline and Churchill were both freemasons, and Gull was the royal doctor. Gull has been described in books and television documentaries as a freemason, yet this is doubtful. The library at Freemasons' Hall is uncertain, and other specialists deny such an allegiance. There was speculation that Stephen had a connection with the Knights Templar Lodge, and that he had been committing the murders with the Duke of Clarence. It was Stephen's view that Gull and Churchill were the

153

guilty men. The report that Abberline sent to Goschen never came to light. At about the same time, Abberline's prevarication allowed important witnesses in the Cleveland Club trial to get away across the Channel. When he was offered early retirement aged only 49 soon after the closure of the Ripper case in 1892, some saw it as a reward for protecting the gentry. The only people likely to know more of the matter were the Home Secretary Henry Matthews and the Prime Minister Lord Salisbury, and both would have obeyed orders. Salisbury, for example, delayed the Cleveland trial for the same reasons as Abberline.

Nor has 100 years of hindsight led to any universal conclusion. Many serious writers with heavily researched views have come to different conclusions. If anything, opinions have become more diverse. Like today's Honours List, certain names find their way on to the roll call to 'add interest'. The Ripper list contains at least two such names, William Gladstone and Charles Dodgson. Recently both made it onto the top two dozen in a poll of suspects, which is a reflection more of the paucity of real suspects than of any possibility of their guilt.

Gladstone was a great Liberal reformer but he was obsessed with reforming prostitutes, which had been an 'interest' of his since university days. He regularly visited the East End to persuade them to take up other work, and sometimes when he was Prime Minister he invited them back to No. 10 for refreshments. We do not know whether they were paid. Benjamin Disraeli is credited with the remark: 'If you are saving fallen women, save one for me.' Eventually this eccentricity became such an embarrassment to his party that he was warned by his colleagues to desist. Gladstone took no notice and continued to wobble on the line between well-meaning innocence and self-gratification. His mission, peculiar as it was, was nevertheless the only reason for his name ever reaching the frame.

The eccentricities of Dodgson were not so harmless, although they were far from making him a serious candidate. He was a clergyman with a most marked preference for little girls. He would cultivate their friendship, photograph them, sometimes undressed, and then abandon them when they reached the age of 13. An extract from an invitation written in the early 1890s illustrates these proclivities: 'If your little girl would like to pay a visit to my little girl we should be very glad to see her and I daresay we could find something to show her.' Dodgson admitted: 'In my old age I have begun to have girlfriends to brighten my lonely life by the sea.' One of them was his model for Alice in *Alice in Wonderland*. He may not have been a paedophile in the worst sense of the word, but his preoccupation was distinctly unhealthy. One of his last protégées commented: 'The Victorian mind saw possible evil in the association of a child of 12 with an old man of 63.' As with Gladstone, it is difficult to see how Dodgson's perverted tastes ever fitted the profile of a mass murderer.

The suggestion that the Duke of Clarence was the Ripper may also seem fanciful, but at the time the rumours were sufficiently strong for the Metropolitan Police to set up a top secret investigation at the Rochester Row police station in Westminster to decide if the Duke could possibly have been the culprit. In *Matriarch*, a study of Queen Mary and the House of Windsor published in 1984, Anne Edwards alludes to this investigation, and to the whispers.

Hundreds of books have been written that relate to the Whitechapel murders and nearly all mention Montague. One that actually indicted him was Daniel Farson's *Jack the Ripper* published in 1972. It is now seen as flawed. It relies on the 'The East End Murderer - I Knew Him' article in Australia that Martin Howells and Keith Skinner have shown to be an irrelevance. It also takes no account of Montague's cricket commitments, which tell so much about his movements and priorities. Even the single reference to Montague playing at Lord's for Winchester College is wrong. It is clear Farson had irritated the College by his continued inquisitiveness and inaccuracy, as the following letter from the Bursar, Ruthven Hall, shows. It was to James Sabben-Clare, a don at the College at the time with responsibilities for 'all things Wykehamical'. Sabben-Clare became headmaster in 1985.

From THE BURSAR, WINCHESTER COLLEGE
22nd March, 1973

Dear James,

Jack the Ripper

Thank you for your letter of 20th March enclosing Daniel Farson's letter of 15th March, which I return herewith.

I really feel we have gone far enough in providing titbits of information about Druitt. I would be willing to go further if it would help to discover the truth about him, but I cannot see that this would be achieved by providing reproductions of his handwriting or of his carved name in School. This sort of thing seems to me to have only a journalistic attraction and would no doubt involve us in further tiresome requests from newspapers etc. to make further reproductions.

I therefore suggest that we draw a firm line and refuse to provide any further particulars which are not conducive to historical accuracy.

Yours ever,

Ruthven

The school's policy must have softened over the years, as my questions were met with impeccable helpfulness.

Farson tried to claim that Montague was left-handed, hence fitting in with the initial view of the police surgeon that the murderer of Mary Nichols was left-handed. If Montague had been left-handed it would have been mentioned in the *Lillywhite's Cricketers' Annuals*. These included several references to Montague, but made no mention of this trait. Cricket books nearly always point out left-handedness. All Farson had to go on was that Montague was a good Fives player and therefore needed to be competent with his left hand. Further, Farson claimed that Montague had some medical or surgical knowledge, which was not the case. Finally, much of Farson's case is based on the Macnaghten notes, which are now also discredited.

Another suggestion that Montague could have been involved came from John Wilding in *Jack the Ripper Revealed*. This was an imaginative tale of how James Stephen recruited Montague, a friend of similar background, to track down and kill Mary Kelly for reasons already explained. He alleged that the five victims all lived close to each other, and drank and gossiped together, so it would be helpful to secure the royal secret if the other four were removed as well. Also it might draw attention away from the real target, Mary Kelly. Stephen and Montague are therefore portrayed as unofficial royal hitmen, preserving the reputation of the monarchy itself. Wilding's case makes no reference to the extent of Montague's cricket activity, the important role it played in his social life, nor the alibis it provided. Once again Macnaghten's speculative notes are used to suppose Montague was homosexual and therefore more malleable to Stephen. Now that so much more is known of Montague's life and character, Wilding's story is most questionable.

The idea of a double act was not unique. The American writer Dr David Abrahamsen put forward James Stephen and the Duke himself, and Stephen went for Dr Gull and Lord Randolph Churchill. The multitude of suspects reflects the uncertainty among police, politicians, writers and indeed everyone else from that day to this. It is much easier to be certain who was not guilty than who was.

In *Jack the Ripper: An Encyclopaedia*, John L. Eddleston examines over a hundred characters, some of whom, such as King Leopold II of Belgium, Mary of Bremen (a male hairdresser), and Edwin Burrows who wore a peaked cap, are not serious suspects at all. Montague is rated at the lowest edge of credibility along with such unknowns as John Foster, an Irishman, Alfred Gray, a vagrant with a tattoo and a Polish Jew known only as Wirtofsky.

Robert Anderson and Melville Macnaghten both believed there were five murders, culminating in that of Mary Kelly. Anderson said in his biography: 'The last and most horrible of that maniac's crimes was committed in a house in Miller's Court on the 9 November.' Macnaghten stated in February 1894: 'Now the Whitechapel murderer had five victims and five victims only.' However this was not a completely accepted truth either then or now. There were at least three other candidates. Martha Tabram, who sometimes used the names Emma or Turner, was killed on 7 August

1888 in George Yard, off the Whitechapel Road. She was a prostitute, and at the time most people believed she was the first victim of Jack the Ripper. This was the time when Montague played five days of cricket as part of the Bournemouth Cricket Week in 4–11 August, including 6 August. It scarcely left time for a 200-mile round dash to fit in a murder. Tabram offered her services mostly to soldiers, particularly those stationed at the Tower of London. She was last seen picking up two of them, and was found later that night stabbed to death, possibly with a bayonet. After the murder, a girl friend who had been with her attended identity parades at the Tower of London and Wellington Barracks. The friend picked out two men, both of whom had solid alibis, and the inquiry dissolved. Thereafter soldiers stationed at the Tower were not allowed to carry bayonets on leave. The Royal Engineers, the regiment of Montague's brother Edward, were stationed close by at Tower Hamlets, and they put up a reward of £100 and offered fifty men 'either for the protection of the public or for finding out criminals'. For whatever reason, Edward left abruptly for Army duties in Australia following Montague's death.

However, there is a possibility that there was an earlier victim. Emma Smith, a woman of shadowy reputation and wild drinking habits, was attacked by a group of men off Whitechapel Road. She died the next day, 4 April 1888, of her injuries. Detective Constable Walter Dew, who was covering the Whitechapel area at the time, said in his autobiography: 'I have always held that Emma Smith was the first to meet her death at the hands of Jack the Ripper.' Dew went on to achieve lasting fame when he arrested Dr Crippen, the infamous American murderer, in mid-Atlantic. Crippen poisoned his wife, cut up her body, burnt the bones and buried the remains in a cellar. He was hanged in London in 1910. It was because of Smith's murder that the police opened the Whitechapel murders file, which was closed by Macnaghten in 1892.

Following 'the famous five', there were other candidates. On 20 December 1888 Rose Mylett or Davis was killed in Poplar. She had been working the streets, and was garrotted with a rope. The murder was never solved, but it did not bear the hallmarks of the Ripper. There were two further murders over the next two years that had stronger Ripper credentials. On 17 July 1889 Alice McKenzie was murdered off Whitechapel High Street. Again she was a prostitute and her body had been slashed and stabbed. Wynne Baxter was the coroner. As has been detailed earlier, it was significant that Dr Thomas Bond, who assisted in the medical assessment, stated that this murder, too, was the work of 'the same person who committed the former series of Whitechapel murders'.

This was an important view, as Bond had participated in the inquest of Mary Kelly and had written a report on all the murders for Robert Anderson. He believed the five murders were committed by the same person and now there was a sixth. His professional qualifications were excellent. Yet Dr Phillips, who worked on four of the earlier murders, directly disagreed. Such was the disparity of opinion among the best of the medical experts. If Bond was correct and this was the sixth Ripper murder by the same hand, then Montague could not have had anything to do with any of them, since by the time of the sixth he was dead.

The last victim to be included in the Whitechapel murders file was Frances Coles, who was killed on 13 February 1891. Her death conformed to the Ripper pattern in that her body had been cut open in the familiar way, and her usual activities were prostitution and drinking. The policeman who found the body immediately described it as a 'Jack the Ripper job'. This report reached the public, who became very excited when a seaman called Thomas Sadler was arrested. He was well known to Coles, but, after spending time on remand, he was eventually released. The *Spectator* commented that 'it is more than possible, it is almost probable, that she was killed by Jack the Ripper'. Macnaghten did not agree. He attributed the killing of Coles and McKenzie to Sadler, thus conveniently retaining his 'five victims only' theory. Sadler, on release, promptly sailed to South America and was never heard of again.

During the early 1890s the response of sections of the police force and the reaction of the public indicate little conviction that the murderer was either dead, locked in an asylum or had stopped his activities. Macnaghten may have been frustrated by this failure, closed the case and tried to make the best of a bad job by writing his own account which would exonerate everybody except those unable to sue him, or cut short his career. A contemporary copy of *The Times* said there were nine victims; Ronald Pearsall thought there were eight. Others have claimed up to twelve. Even the dates of some of the murders vary.

Out of so much uncertainty it is invidious to draw a guilty verdict. From this morass Montague's reputation deserves to emerge if not unblemished, at least with some credit. The only blot was something he did to be dismissed from Valentine's school. It was an error that filled him with remorse at his own stupidity. His social and professional life unravelled at a stroke, and even those used to a more liberated lifestyle failed to support him – not because of the severity of the offence, whatever it may have been, but because he was not quite far enough up the social scale to merit their help. Had he been of higher social standing, there was no misdemeanour that he could not have survived.

The number of his friends and acquaintances who have been mentioned in connection with Jack the Ripper is not surprising. Montague moved in circles covering the Law, the edges of aristocracy, university intelligentsia, the medical profession and cricket. Sometimes these circles overlapped. Men such as Lord Wimborne, Lord Harris, James Stephen, Harry Wilson, Evelyn Ruggles-Brise, John Dalton, Nicholas 'Felix' Wanostrocht, Lord Darnley and Alexander Webbe would always be welcome in upper-class society. It was these sort of people who, if not at the very top of the ladder, certainly had direct connections with people who were.

Montague may have been a 'nearly man'. He could not quite make the biggest league in his own right. He could not get a top degree at Oxford and he played his cricket for New College but did not get a Blue. He was a schoolmaster but did little teaching, and could not quite succeed as a barrister. He was a very good club cricketer but not a first-class one; he was a member of MCC but never played at Lord's. He might have wished to have become an Apostle, but his Oxford background debarred him, so could not get beyond the 'embryo' stage. Caught in the intrigue of the highest levels of government, royalty and society, not to mention the Law and the medical profession, Montague may have been an ingénu. The reality is that during his life he was never questioned by the police and he was never on any list of suspects. Nor was he prone to violence, he had no recorded interest in knives and he probably only had the vaguest idea where Whitechapel was. His territory was the Inns of Court, the cloisters of Winchester and Oxford and the cricket field.

The evidence is that until the last week of his life he led an enjoyable, privileged and blameless existence. For his name finally to be removed from an association with the Whitechapel murders would be long overdue. Indeed, it should never have been made in the first place. It would also bring a small relief to the MCC, a club to which he was so proud to belong. Questioned about Montague's connection with the club, the curator at Lord's for 35 years, Stephen Green, wrote in the finest tradition of MCC loftiness: 'I have heard the rumour about M.J. Druitt, but I hope an MCC member would not commit such crimes.' Indeed not.

Three of England's great institutions contributed suspects, if the list is viewed in its loosest sense. Of the schools, Eton led the way with four: the Duke of Clarence, James Stephen, Randolph Churchill and William Gladstone. Oxford supplied Montague, Churchill, Charles Dodgson and Gladstone, and the MCC was well represented. It included in its membership the Duke, Conan Doyle and Montague. Other cricket clubs with at least one suspect included Portsmouth, Incogniti, Grayshott, Blackheath, I Zingari, Norwood and the Butterflies.

The death of Montague remains shrouded in mystery. From what we are allowed to know of the inquest (the official papers have been lost), it was a perfunctory procedure. Key witnesses were not called, proper questions were not asked and no attempt was made to find out Montague's last movements. The verdict of suicide was too quick and too convenient. Today with a full inquest procedure an open verdict would be possible, with everything that implies, including legitimate questions about murder. However, it was 1889, and such matters as inquests could be manipulated. The truth may never be known, but an interesting and happy life does not deserve to be remembered with accusations of mass murder on account of being dismissed from a school. The author James Tully says of Montague: 'Druitt simply does not fit the key criteria found by modern psychological profiling to be common to serial killers.'

In 2000 a professor of criminology at Texas State University, Kim Rossmo, published his findings using 'Geographic Profiling'. Rossmo had developed a computer programme called Rigel, and it processed information based on the location of a crime. From this information it claimed to identify, very closely, the home address of the culprit. The places of the five murders were fed into Rigel, and the answer came back that the Ripper lived in Flower and Dean Street or Thrawl Street – the worst part of Whitechapel. The Rigel identification process has support from the UK's National Crime and Operations Faculty in Hampshire.

It seems that with every modern process of analysis, be it DNA, graphology, psychological profiling or geographic profiling, the more the innocence of Montague is confirmed.

Montague was no more a murderer than the aforementioned Mary of Bremen, but he did have a victim that day on 8 September 1888. In fact he had three. All were Christophersons and all were bowled. There were to be no more victims on or off the field. The evidence gained from a study of Montague's life leads incontrovertibly to the conclusion that, when the dots are joined up, the writing says that Montague Druitt, should be remembered as one of the pioneers of the modern-day Blackheath Cricket Club, and for no other reason.

Montague deserves the last word. On that December night did he go to The Osiers? Perhaps, in dismay at being abandoned by his erstwhile colleagues, he sat on his own and reviewed his plight. Maybe he remembered his carefree Oxford days and a little of the Latin that had earned him a degree. He could have scribbled on an Osiers letterhead 'nothi ad siccandum suspenderunt me' or 'the bastards have hung me out to dry'. Such a note was never found. If he did not write it, he should have done.

APPENDIX

Scorecards of a Cricketer

About fifty scorecards still exist that detail matches in which Montague played, from his time at Winchester to his last game at Blackheath on 8 September 1888. This is a selection of those scorecards. Many record good performances and several show when he played with or against some of the top-class cricketers who are mentioned in this book.

Winchester College*	v.	Eton College	June 1876
The Oxford Freshmen's Match			April 1877
The Oxford Seniors' Match			April 1880
Blackheath*	v.	Incogniti	July 1881
Dorset*	v.	Incogniti	August 1881
Bournemouth	v.	Incogniti*	August 1881
Sidmouth	v.	Incogniti*	August 1881
Kingston Park*	v.	Incogniti	August 1882
Torquay	v.	Incogniti*	August 1882
Winchester College	v.	Butterflies*	June 1883
Kingston Park*	v.	Incogniti	July 1883
Kingston Park*	v.	Ishmaelites	August 1883
Plymouth Garrison	v.	Incogniti*	August 1883
Blackheath*	v.	G. G. Hearne's XI	April 1886
Blackheath*	v.	Band of Brothers	June 1886
Harrow School	v.	MCC*	June 1886
Bexley	v.	Blackheath*	June 1886
Clergy of England	v.	MCC*	July 1886
Blackheath*	v.	Surrey Club and Ground	May 1887
Blackheath*	v.	Incogniti	May 1887
Blackheath	v.	O. Wykehamists*	June 1887
Blackheath*	v.	MCC	July 1887

Bryn-y-Neuadd	v.	Incogniti*	August 1887
Blackheath*	v.	Royal Artillery	June 1888
Blackheath*	v.	Bickley Park	June 1888
Blackheath*	v.	The Christopherson Brothers	September 1888

* Indicates the side that Montague played for.

WINCHESTER COLLGE V. ETON COLLEGE
Played at Ridding Field, Winchester, 23 and 24 June 1876
(Umpires: G. Lee and R. Thoms)

ETON COLLEGE	1ST INNS	
W.F. Forbes	c. Moon, b. Rooper	33
J.E.K. Studd	b. Druitt	4
H. Whitfield	c. Moon, b. Thornton	13
E.G. Ruggles-Brise	c. Wilson, b. Rooper	34
Hon. Ivo Bligh	b. Fort	73
H. Goodhart	b. Rooper	12
L. Bury	b. Druitt	3
C.W. Foley	c. Pritchard, b. Rooper	35
G. Forbes	b. Rooper	7
G. Portal	not out	2
C.M. Smith	b. Thornton	6
	b. 7, l.b. 5, w 6	18
		240

WINCHESTER COLLEGE	1ST INNS		2ND INNS	
F.S. Baines	c. Whitfeld, b. Smith	4	c. Bury, b. Portal	0
W.A. Thornton	not out	31	b. Bury	22
R.B.A. Pritchard	c. Whitfeld, b. Smith	0	b. Smith	0
J. Eyre	run out	0	b. W.F. Forbes	16
J.A. Fort	b. Smith	5	b. W.F. Forbes	5
A.W. Moon	b. W.F. Forbes	7	b. W.F. Forbes	0
A.H. Rooper	c. Bligh, b. W.F. Forbes	3	run out	4
W.R. Sheldon	c. Bligh, b. Smith	0	not out	10
H.W.B. Bird	c. Whitfeld, b. Smith	11	c. Smith, b. W.F. Forbes	0
M.J. Druitt	run out	10	b. Whitfeld	2
S.J. Wilson	b. Portal	0	b. W.F. Forbes	0
	l.b. 2, n.b. 1	3	b. 3, l.b. 2, w 1, n.b. 2	8
		74		**67**

WINCHESTER COLLEGE BOWLING

	Balls	Runs	Wickets
Rooper	284	83	5
Druitt	192	67	2
Thornton	121	50	2
Fort	36	22	1

ETON COLLEGE BOWLING

	Balls	Runs	Wickets	Balls	Runs	Wickets
W.F. Forbes	116	32	2	79	7	5
Smith	120	39	5	52	18	1
Portal	7	0	1	32	20	1
Bury				44	10	1
Whitfeld				12	3	1

Eton won by an innings and 99 runs.

THE OXFORD FRESHMEN'S MATCH
Played on the Magdelene Ground, 27 and 28 April 1877
Thirteen-a-side played, with the following result:

MR E.T. HIRST'S SIDE	1ST INNS		2ND INNS	
W.J.M. Hughes, Esq.	c. and b. Key	0	b. Druitt	17
V.F. Hornby, Esq.	b. Horner	12	b. Key	0
H.F. Blaine, Esq.	b. Key	2	c. Greene, b. Druitt	7
A.S. Bennett, Esq.	c. and b. Key	0	c. Greene, b. Druitt	1
E.T. Hirst, Esq.	c. Greene, b. Key	3	c. Greene, b. Druitt	2
E. Ruggles-Brise, Esq.	b. Druitt	6	b. Druitt	20
E. Alington, Esq.	b. Horner	0	b. Horner	7
H. Harrison, Esq.	b. Horner	0	c. Waddington, b. Horner	0
R.P. Higgs, Esq.	b. Horner	4	b. Horner	0
F.G. Jellicoe, Esq.	b. Key	0	c. Druitt, b. Horner	2
G.C. Robertson, Esq.	c. Turner, b. Key	0	not out	3
G.A. Hicks, Esq.	c. Druitt, b. Horner	12	c. Fowler, b. Horner	6
Owen, Esq.	not out	11	b. Horner	5
	b. 4, l.b. 1, w 1	6	b. 3, l.b. 5, w 4	12
		56		82

MR H. FOWLER'S SIDE	1ST INNS		2ND INNS	
J.M. Hare, Esq.	b. Jellicoe	10	b. Jellicoe	16
W.H.P. Rowe, Esq.	b. Jellicoe	0	b. Jellicoe	14
R.B.A. Pritchard, Esq.	c. and b. Higgs	10		
A.D. Greene, Esq.	b. Higgs	2	not out	15
H. Fowler, Esq.	b. Jellicoe	16	not out	18
J. Peddle, Esq.	b. Jellicoe	6		
E. Waddington, Esq.	b. Jellicoe	2		
F.A. Govett, Esq.	b. Harrison	0		
A. Cooper-Key, Esq.	b. Jellicoe	9		
W. Were, Esq.	not out	2		
M.J. Druitt, Esq.	b. Jellicoe	2	b. Jellicoe	11
C.E. Horner, Esq.	b. Owen	1		
G.E. Turner, Esq.	b. Jellicoe	0		
	b. 4, l.b. 1	5	l.b. 3	3
		65		77

BOWLING BY MR FOWLER'S MEN

	Overs	Mdns	Runs	Wide	Wkts	Overs	Mdns	Runs	Wide	Wkts
Mr Horner	18	7	20	–	5	22.2	16	10	–	6
Mr Druitt	8	5	5	–	1	31	17	30	3	5
Mr Key	24	15	21	1	6	10	5	13	1	1
Mr Turner	2	1	4	–	–					
Mr Greene						16	5	17	–	–

BOWLING BY MR HIRST'S MEN

	Overs	Mdns	Runs	Wide	Wkts	Overs	Mdns	Runs	Wide	Wkts
Mr Jellicoe	32	15	25	–	8	25	15	25	–	3
Mr Higgs	17	9	27	–	2	9	2	14	–	–
Mr Harrison	8	5	3	–	1					
Mr Owen	6	4	5	–	1	8	1	19	–	–
Mr Hicks						8	2	16	–	–

Mr Fowler's side won by 4 runs.

(Mr Jellicoe, Mr Fowler, Mr Greene and Mr Waddington played against Cambridge at Lord's.)

THE OXFORD SENIORS' MATCH
Played 26, 27 and 28 April 1880

MR R.L. KNIGHT'S SIDE	1ST INNS		2ND INNS	
E.L. Colebrook, Esq. (E)	b. Druitt	36	b. Horner	7
W.H. Patterson, Esq. (P)	c. Trevor, b. Druitt	54	run out	81
E.H. Hill, Esq. (O)	c. Trevor, b. Druitt	20	b. Jones	25
R.L. Knight, Esq. (C)	b. Trevor	4	c. Trevor, b. Wallace	18
B. Fitzgerald, Esq. (U)	c. Baines, b. Trevor	4	c. sub, b. Wallace	7
W.H. Heale, Esq. (B)	b. Horner	12	b. Horner	29
H.F. Fox, Esq. (U)	b. Jones	9	b. Horner	0
C.G. Gutteres, Esq. (O)	b. Horner	7	not out	24
W.H. Mansfield, Esq. (P)	b. Jones	42	c. and b. Trevor	18
R. Lubbock, Esq. (Ba)	c. Pritchard, b. Horner	13		
A.A. Mackenzie, Esq. (Br)	not out	3	not out	1
W.B. Brown, Esq. (Br)	b. Horner	0		
	b. 6, l.b. 3	9	b. 8, l.b. 9, w 2	19
		213		**229**

MR HORNER'S SIDE	1ST INNS	
R.B. Pritchard, Esq. (N)	b. Knight	0
T.G. Ridley, Esq. (E)	b. Knight	11
A.H. Trevor, Esq. (C)	c. Heale, b. Patterson	142
C.H. Hodgson, Esq. (H)	b. Patterson	42
W. Wallace, Esq. (W)	b. Patterson	17
F.S. Baines, Esq. (U)	b. Patterson	0
W.E. Dunsford, Esq. (N)	b. Knight	12
J. Eyre, Esq. (Ch)	not out	76
A.W. Moon, Esq. (O)	lbw, b. Knight	0
C.E. Horner, Esq. (Br)	b. Mackenzie	10
O. Jones, Esq. (J)	c. and b. Patterson	35
M.J. Druitt, Esq. (N)	absent	–
	b. 30, l.b. 5, w 9	44
		389

BOWLING BY MR HORNER'S SIDE

	Overs	Mdns	Runs	Wkts	Overs	Mdns	Runs	Wkts
Mr Druitt	35	19	43	3				
Mr Horner	44.2	20	56	4	40	22	58	3
Mr Jones	39	19	50	2	34	15	55	1
Mr Hodgson	3	1	14	–	7	3	12	–
Mr Ridley	8	5	9	–	9	3	9	–
Mr Trevor	9	4	32	2	20	3	46	1
Mr Wallace					14	8	19	2
Mr Eyre					8	5	8	–

BOWLING BY MR R.L. KNIGHT'S SIDE

	Overs	Mdns	Runs	Wkts
Mr Knight	54	10	135	4
Mr Brown	13	5	18	–
Mr Patterson	53	15	116	5
Mr Mackenzie	23	7	32	1
Mr Lubbock	20	4	40	–

The heavy scoring caused the match to be drawn.

BLACKHEATH V. INCOGNITI
Played at Blackheath on 6 July 1881
(Umpires: G. Lee and R. Thoms.)

INCOGNITI			BLACKHEATH MORDEN		
H. Ross	b. A. Penn	5	F. Penn	c. Friend, b. Palmer	21
G.K. Anderson	b. Druitt	5	G. Stokes	b. Palmer	6
E.C. Friend	b. Druitt	3	L. Stokes	b. Palmer	2
H.J. Hill	b. Druitt	17	F.S. Ireland	c. Hemmings, b. Palmer	39
T.C.A. Barrett	lbw, b. A. Penn	0	J.E. Shaw	b. Palmer	17
P. Hilton	b. Ireland	10	F.H. Lacey	c. Hilton, b. Friend	1
A.W.L. Hemming	c. Christopherson, b. A. Penn	10	A. Penn	c. Fletcher, b. Palmer	7
W. Fletcher	st. Prior, b. A. Penn	0	E.H. Rodwell	not out	14
F.J.O. Thomas	b. Druitt	1	F.W. Prior	st. Hilton, b. Barrett	10
O. Thomas	not out	6	M.J. Druitt	c. sub, b. Palmer	1
G. Palmer	b. Ireland	0	S. Christopherson	b. Barrett	5
	b. 4, l.b. 1, w 1	6		b. 1, l.b. 2, w 1	4
		63			127

Blackheath Morden won by 64 runs.

DORSET V. INCOGNITI
Played at Dorchester on 3 and 4 August 1881

INCOGNITI	1ST INNS		2ND INNS	
H.J. Hill	c. Hawkey, b. Cassan	2	b. Cassan	0
E.T. Noyes	c. and b. Druitt	34	b. Bastard	0
C. Awdry	b. Cassan	3	b. Cassan	50
T.R. Hine-Haydock	c. Wilson, b. Druitt	10	b. Bastard	8
J.S. Udal	b. Druitt	2	b. Bastard	0
W.S. Trollope	run out	0	b. Cassan	11
E. Giberne	b. Druitt	0	b. Bastard	3
Capt. P.K.L. Beaver	c. sub, b. Bastard	0	b. Druitt	24
A.W.L. Hemming	lbw, b. Wilson	8	c. Bewes, b. Cassan	19
J.C. Moberly	not out	8	b. Bastard	5
H.P. Thomas	b. Bastard	3	not out	0
	b. 3, n.b. 1	4	b. 1	1
		74		121

DORSET	1ST INNS	
C.H. Hodgson	lbw, b. Hine-Haycock	17
A.G. Bewes	c. and b. Moberly	65
C.F. Sweet	c. Thomas, b. Hine-Haycock	12
T.W. Wilson	c. Giberne, b. Hine-Haycock	22
Hon. C. Finch	b. Trollope	2
M.J. Druitt	c. Hill, b. Moberly	64
E.T. Whitfield-Hawkey	b. Trollope	17
T. Raven	not out	26
E.W. Bastard	c. Thomas, b. Trollope	1
Revd S.E. Nicholls	b. Hill	18
E. Cassan	b. Hill	0
	b. 6, l.b. 2, w 3	11
		255

Dorset won by an innings and 60 runs.

BOURNEMOUTH V. INCOGNITI
Played at Bournemouth on 5 and 6 August 1881

BOURNEMOUTH	1ST INNS		2ND INNS	
H. Hanger	b. Druitt	12	c. Noyes, b. Trollope	0
Tuck	c. Hine-Haycock, b. Druitt	14	b. Druitt	2
F.E. Lacey	c. and b. Trollope	4	absent	0
T.B. Scott	b. Trollope	4	b. Trollope	13
A.F. Gurney	b. Druitt	19	c. Hine-Haycock, b. Trollope	3
Revd N. Thompson	b. Druitt	0	not out	7
Revd E.K. Browne	b. Druitt	0	b. Trollope	0
G. Fletcher	c. and b. Druitt	0	b. Druitt	10
C. Rendall	b. Druitt	5	c. Hemming, b. Druitt	0
Revd J. Byrne	b. Druitt	1	b. Druitt	0
H. Lacey	not out	3	b. Trollope	13
	b. 4, l.b. 5, w 1	10	b. 1, l.b. 2, n.b. 1	4
		72		52

INCOGNITI	1ST INNS	
Capt. P.K.L. Beaver	c. Tuck, b. F. Lacey	0
H.P. Thomas	c. Tuck, b. F. Lacey	5
W.S. Trollope	b. Byrne	20
C.T. Awdry	c. Tuck, b. F. Lacey	11
T.R. Hine-Haycock	not out	96
E.T. Noyes	c. Tuck, b. F. Lacey	6
M.J. Druitt	c. Gurney, b. Thompson	14
H.J. Hill	c. Hanger, b. F. Lacey	31
E. Giberne	c. Tuck, b. Rendall	35
J.C. Moberly	b. H. Lacey	38
A.W.L. Hemming	c. F. Lacey, b. H. Lacey	0
	b. 4, l.b. 2, w 1, n.b. 1	8
		264

Incogniti won by an innings and 140 runs.

SIDMOUTH V. INCOGNITI
Played at Sidmouth on 12 and 13 August 1881

SIDMOUTH	1ST INNS	
W.H. Fowler	c. Hemming, b. Druitt	7
D.F. Douglas	c. Monkland, b. Trollope	1
W.A. Thornton	c. Druitt, b. Hill	53
T.R. Hine-Haycock	c. and b. Druitt	0
F.S. Ireland	c. Awdry, b. Trollope	56
Revd R.T. Thornton	c. Beaver, b. Hill	54
R.D. Vizard	b. Fox	32
R.W. Hine-Haycock	not out	0
A.T. McKenzie	c. Hemming, b. Monkland	12
S. Richardson	c. Trollope, b. Fox	0
F.H. Ingham	b. Fox	0
	b. 7, l.b. 11, n.b. 1	19
		234

INCOGNITI	1ST INNS		2ND INNS	
W.S. Trollope	b. W. Thornton	17	absent	0
E.T. Noyes	b. R. Thornton	5	c. T. Hine-Haycock, b. W. Thornton	15
Capt. P.K.L. Beaver	run out	1	b. Ireland	1
F.G. Monkland	c. T. Hine-Haycock, b. R. Thornton	7	c. Richardson, b. Ireland	20
H.J. Hill	c. Vizard, b. Ireland	20	c. and b. W. Thornton	0
C. Awdry	b. R. Thornton	1	c. R. Thornton, b. Ireland	23
M.J. Druitt	c. Ingham, b. Ireland	25	b. R. Thornton	2
E. Giberne	c. and b. Ireland	0	c. Vizard, b. Ingham	21
H.P. Thomas	not out	22	b. W. Thornton	15
A.W.L. Hemming	b. R. Thornton		c. and b. Ireland	10
T.C. Fox	c. Fowler, b. Ireland	0	not out	2
	b. 3, l.b. 3, w 1	7	b. 7, l.b. 10	17
		105		**126**

Sidmouth won by an innings and 3 runs.

KINGSTON PARK V. INCOGNITI
Played at Dorchester on 4 and 5 August 1882

INCOGNITI			KINGSTON PARK		
H.J. Hill	b. Forman	54	T.W. Wilson	b. Hornby	29
J. Smith	c. sub, b. Bastard	1	A.E. Gibson	c. Awdry, b. Hornby	4
W. Winter	c. Fisher, b. Lacey	7	M.J. Druitt	c. Hemming, b. Moberly	23
E. Lesse	b. Wilson	28	F.E. Lacey	c. Morris, b. Smith	77
C. Awdry	c. Lacey, b. Wilson	16	Revd A.F. Forman	c. Lesse, b. Martyn	110
F.V. Hornby	b. Bastard	73	F.B. Fisher	b. Hornby	90
E. Giberne	b. Wilson	11	Parmenter	c. Lesse, b. Winter	13
O.B. Martyn	b. Druitt	57	E. Bastard	st. Morris, b. Smith	18
J.C. Moberly	c. Lacey, b. Bastard	12	H. Kindersley	c. Lesse, b. Smith	8
A.W.L. Hemming	b. Bastard	16	Capt. A.E. Mansel	not out	7
W. Morris	not out	9	M. Thackeray	not out	1
	b. 12, l.b. 9, w 1, n.b. 2	24		b. 10, l.b. 6, w 3, n.b. 4	23
		308			**403**

The match was drawn.

TORQUAY V. INCOGNITI
Played at Torquay on 7 and 8 August 1882

INCOGNITI	1ST INNS		2ND INNS	
J. Smith	b. Webber	3	b. Sanders	17
O.B. Martyn	c. sub, b. Relf	2	c. Poland, b. Relf	1
D.D. Pontiflex	c. Mapleton, b. Relf	102	c. Mapleton, b. Relf	28
E. Lesse	c. Thomas, b. Coxhead	40	b. Relf	4
W. Lindsay	b. Coxhead	0	c. Thomas, b. Coxhead	3
G.L. King	c. Relf, b. Webber	7	run out	12
M.J. Druitt	c. Webber, b. Relf	0	st. Mapleton, b. Relf	15
C. Awdry	not out	19	run out	6
E. Giberne	c. Ridley, b. Relf	6	c. Poland, b. Webber	0
P.V. Turner	c. and b. Relf	0	b. Relf	12
A.F. Robinson	absent	0	not out	0
	b. 13, l.b. 7	20	b. 5, l.b. 1	6
		199		**104**

TORQUAY	1ST INNS		2ND INNS	
F.W. Poland	c. Turner, b. Druitt	64	b. Druitt	14
J.J. Cross	b. Druitt	1	b. Druitt	5
H.B. Mapleton	b. Smith	7		
Lieut. F.O. Thomas, RN	c. Turner, b. Smith	14	st. King, b. Turner	33
F.T. Welman	b. Pontifex	16	not out	9
E.J. Sanders	c. Smith, b. Druitt	20		
F.C. Coxhead	b. Pontifex	16	not out	29
R.B. Webber	b. Druitt	16		
H.W. Ridley	c. Martyn, b. Smith	11	b. Smith	14
Lieut. S. Login, RN	b. Smith	0		
H. Morris	not out	2		
Relf	c. sub, b. Druitt	0		
	b. 11, l.b. 6, w 2	19	b. 2, l.b. 6, w 6, n.b. 3	17
		186		**121**

Torquay won by 6 wickets.

WINCHESTER COLLEGE V. BUTTERFLIES
Played at Winchester on 14 June 1883

BUTTERFLIES	1ST INNS		2ND INNS	
C.R. Seymour	c. Watson, b. Nicholls	0	c. Humphry, b. Haviland	18
J. Eyre	c. Watney, b. Swayne	16	c. Ricketts, b. Watney	10
A.H. Trevor	c. Watney, b. Swayne	5	c. Ricketts, b. Humphry	4
W.A. Thornton	c. Nicholls, b. Swayne	12		
E.H. Hardcastle	c. Watney, b. Nicholls	5	c. Nicholls, b. Watney	3
W.W. Whitmore	st. Cobb, b. Swayne	3	not out	7
Revd J.G. Crowdy	c. Majendie, b. Nicholls	5	b. Watney	18
M.J. Druitt	c. Ingram, b. Nicholls	1	c. Ingram, b. Ricketts	3
Capt. Frederick	st. Cobb, b. Nicholls	9	c. Watney, b. Humphry	13
Lord Eskdaile	c. Watney, b. Nicholls	4	c. Majendie, b. Haviland	2
A.J. Webbe	not out	7		
J.M.F. Fuller	b. Nicholls	11		
	b. 1	1	b. 2	2
		79		80

WINCHESTER COLLEGE	1ST INNS	
A.R. Cobb	c. Trevor, b. Thornton	24
F.M. Ingram	c. Thornton, b. Webbe	7
P. Humphry	c. Druitt, b. Hardcastle	16
G.W. Ricketts	b. Thornton	10
E.B. Hills	b. Thornton	0
A.L. Watson	b. Druitt	3
D. Watney	c. Trevor, b. Eskdaile	5
C.L. Budd	c. Fuller, b. Hardcastle	31
H.G. Majendie	c. Whitmore, b. Thornton	0
B.E. Nicholls	c. Crowdy, b. Eskdaile	6
J.M. Swayne	c. Thornton, b. Webbe	9
F.H. Haviland	not out	3
	l.b. 4, w 1, n.b. 1	6
		120

The match was drawn.

KINGSTON PARK V. INCOGNITI
Played at Kingston Park on 30 and 31 July 1883

INCOGNITI	1ST INNS		2ND INNS	
W. Winter	b. Druitt	0	c. and b. Druitt	28
J. Smith	c. Forman, b. Druitt	8	b. Kelsey	4
S.W. Scott	b. Druitt	27	c. Fookes, b. Fisher	0
Capt. Curtis, RA	b. Druitt	5	b. Fisher	25
E. Lesse	b. Druitt	0	c. Fookes, b. Monro	0
O.B. Martyn	b. Fisher	16	c. Lushington, b. Druitt	16
A.T. Thring	c. and b. Fisher	3	b. Druitt	4
E. Giberne	b. Druitt	13	c. and b. Kelsey	2
W. Morris	not out	17	c. Fort, b. Kelsey	20
A.W.L. Hemming	c. Forman, b. Druitt	2	b. Druitt	3
P. Bevan	run out	0	not out	2
	b. 3, l.b. 1, w 1	5	b. 5, l.b. 3, w 1	9
		96		113

KINGSTON PARK	1ST INNS		2ND INNS	
J.A. Fort	b. Scott	3	b. Curtis	4
W. Fookes	lbw, b. Scott	0	b. Curtis	2
F.B. Fisher	b. Scott	38	c. Giberne, b. Curtis	0
Revd A.F.E. Forman	b. Scott	0	c. Morris, b. Scott	9
G.W. Lushington	b. Scott	0	b. Curtis	40
M.J. Druitt	st. Morris, b. Scott	2	run out	27
E. Kindersley	b. Scott	2	b. Curtis	17
O. Wynne	c. Martyn, b. Scott	5	c. Scott, b. Curtis	11
C.C. Monro	c. and b. Scott	0	not out	11
Capt. Kelsey	not out	1	c. Bevan, b. Curtis	5
R. Wynyard	absent	0	not out	8
	b. 1, l.b. 2, n.b. 1	4	b. 14, l.b. 5, w 1, n.b. 1	21
		55		155

Kingston Park won by one wicket.

KINGSTON PARK V. ISHMAELITES
Played at Kingston Park on 6 and 7 August 1883

ISHMAELITES	1ST INNS		2ND INNS	
R. Grouse	b. Druitt	2	c. Fisher, b. Parmenter	1
M.J.F. Brackenbury	b. Druitt	0	b. Parmenter	1
E.C. Evelyn	b. Druitt	6	not out	5
F.E. Haviland	b. Druitt	26	c. Fort, b. Druitt	1
H.R. Heatley	c. Fisher, b. Druitt	26	lbw, b. Parmenter	16
F.D. Gaddum	c. Kindersley, b. Druitt	3		
E.D. Hake	b. Druitt	72		
G. Street	b. Druitt	11		
F.H. Haviland	b. Druitt	3	not out	2
L. Easum	b. Druitt	12		
E.L. Heatley	not out	28	b. Druitt	5
	b. 13, l.b. 3, w 3, n.b. 1	20	b. 1, w 1	2
		209		**33**

KINGSTON PARK	1ST INNS	
M.J. Druitt	b. Easum	3
F.B. Fisher	not out	110
G.W. Lushington	b. Easum	30
C. Kindersley	c. Grouse, b. Gaddum	1
Major Churchill	c. Brackenbury, b. Easum	0
J. Parmenter	c. Evelyn, b. Easum	15
Col. Traell	b. F.E. Haviland	29
J.A. Fort	c. H.R. Heatley, b. Gaddum	21
E. Kindersley	st. H.R. Heatley, b. Gaddum	0
C. Monro	b. Gaddum	2
A.E. Mansel	run out	0
	b. 7, l.b. 1, w 1	9
		220

The match was drawn.

PLYMOUTH GARRISON V. INCOGNITI
Played at Plymouth on 13 and 14 August 1883

PLYMOUTH GARRISON	1ST INNS		2ND INNS	
Lieut. Currie, RA	c. Giberne, b. Horner	8	c. Pontifex, b. Druitt	0
Lieut. Wilbraham (82nd)	b. Druitt	12	b. Druitt	3
H. Lockwood	b. Curtis	22	retired hurt	8
Lieut. Calley, RA	run out	15	c. Martyn, b. Horner	33
Lieut. Heneage (74th)	b. Curtis	5	b. Curtis	2
Lieut. Callaghan, RN	b. Druitt	7	c. Hemming, b. Horner	1
Lieut. Wilson, RN	c. Gripper, b. Horner	2	b. Druitt	3
Smith	b. Druitt	6	c. Pontifex, b. Horner	0
Major Kay, RMLI	b. Druitt	22	c. Pontifex, b. Druitt	21
Corp. Henderson (74th)	not out	2	b. Druitt	7
Lieut. Murphy (82nd)	b. Druitt	0	not out	0
	b. 5, l.b. 4	9	b. 4, l.b. 7	11
		110		**89**

INCOGNITI	1ST INNS	
Capt. Curtis	lbw, b. Smith	14
E. Gripper	run out	0
E. Leese	c. and b. Smith	123
D.D. Pontifex	c. Kay, b. Callaghan	85
O.B. Martyn	b. Callaghan	29
M.J. Druitt	b. Currie	30
P.V. Turner	b. Smith	15
C.E. Horner	not out	24
E. Giberne	c. Kay, b. Wilbraham	39
W. Winter	absent hurt	0
A.W.L. Hemming	b. Callaghan	4
	b. 13, l.b. 4, w 3, n.b. 2	22
		385

Incogniti won by an innings and 186 runs.

BLACKHEATH V. G.G. HEARNE'S XI
Played at The Rectory Field on 26 April 1886

G.G. HEARNE'S XI			BLACKHEATH		
E.B. Ormerod	b. S. Christopherson	0	F.H. Lacey	c. Wooton, b. G.G. Hearne	36
F. Hearne	c. Dale, b. S. Christopherson	17	G. Stokes	c. G.G. Hearne, b. A. Hearne	3
P. Christopherson	b. S. Christopherson	0	S. Christopherson	c. G.G. Hearne, b. A. Hearne	22
G.G. Hearne	c. Ireland, b. S. Christopherson	0	L. Stokes	c. F. Hearne, b. H. Hearne	2
G.F. Hearne	b. S. Christopherson	0	J.D. Cruickshank	b. A. Hearne	1
Wootton	b. S. Christopherson	16	C.L. Hemmerde	b. A. Hearne	4
A. Hearne	b. Druitt	26	M.J. Druitt	c. Pentecost, b. A. Hearne	7
H. Hearne	c. S. Christopherson, b. Dale	15	F.S. Ireland	b. A. Hearne	0
W. Hearne	b. Hemmerde	11	J.M. Dale	c. Pentecost, b. A. Hearne	4
Pentecost	run out	3	Revd J.W. Marshall	not out	0
G. Kibble	not out	3	G.R. Hutchinson	c. Ormerod, b. G.G. Hearne	0
	Extras	9		Extras	–
		100			**79**

This was the inaugural match at The Rectory Field ground.
G.G. Hearne's XI won by 21 runs.

BLACKHEATH V. BAND OF BROTHERS
Played at The Rectory Field on 5 June 1886

BLACKHEATH			BAND OF BROTHERS		
L. Stokes	run out	0	Lord Harris	b. Druitt	14
G. Stokes	c. Tonge, b. Aste	15	W.H. Patterson	lbw, b. Druitt	11
F. Stokes	ht wkt, b. Aste	5	J.N. Tonge	b. Druitt	1
F.H. Lacey	b. Aste	6	F.A. McKinnon	c. Sid Christopherson, b. F. Stokes	4
M.J. Druitt	c. D'aeth, b. Patterson	41	T.R. Hine-Haycock	c. Prior, b. Sid Christopherson	4
F.S. Ireland	ht wkt, b. Hine-Haycock	56	R.S. Jones	b. Druitt	1
R.P. Sewell	b. Lord Harris	52	J. Aste	b. Sid Christopherson	15
K. Christopherson	b. Hine-Haycock	8	M.P. Betts	not out	2
Stan Christopherson	not out	40	M.A. Smith-Masker	c. Stan Christopherson, b. F. Stokes	4
F.W. Prior	b. Patterson	0	G. D'aeth	b. F. Stokes	0
Sid Christopherson	st. Hine-Haycock, b. Patterson	8	W.L. Pemberton	b. F. Stokes	0
	Extras	19		Extras	16
		250			72

Blackheath won by 178 runs.

HARROW SCHOOL V. MCC AND GROUND
Played at Harrow on 10 June 1886

MCC AND GROUND			THE SCHOOL		
D.H. Barry, Esq.	b. Holmes	11	E. Crawley, Esq.	lbw, b. Burge	0
F. Hearne	c. Crawley, b. MacLaren	48	J.S. Robinson, Esq.	b. Attewell	9
E.M. Lucas, Esq.	b. Gorton	0	L.G. Arbuthnot, Esq.	c. Burge, b. Attewell	11
'J.S.F. Fair' (F. Gore Esq.)	c. Torrens, b. MacLaren	18	M.J. Dauglish, Esq.	b. Morton	19
M.J. Druitt, Esq.	c. Gorton, b. MacLaren	10	W.M. Torrens, Esq.	b. F. Lucas	22
G.R. Burge, Esq.	st. Torrens, b. Warren	31	N.T. Holmes, Esq.	b. Attewell	7
P.H. Morton, Esq.	c. Crawley, b. Ramsay	21	H.F. Kemp, Esq.	b. Morton	6
R.J. McNeill, Esq.	st. Torrens, b. Ramsay	11	R.R. Warren, Esq.	b. Morton	0
Revd F.G.L. Lucas	c. MacLaren, b. Gorton	16	E.G. Raphael, Esq.	b. Morton	0
Attewell	b. Gorton	1	R.H. Gorton, Esq.	not out	14
I.D. Walker, Esq.	not out	1	J.A. MacLaren, Esq.	b. Morton	1
H.E. Rhodes, Esq.	absent	0	A.D. Ramsay, Esq.	b. Attewell	18
	b. 5, l.b. 2	7		b. 7, l.b. 2, w 1	11
		175			**118**

MCC and Ground won by 57 runs.

BEXLEY V. BLACKHEATH
Played at Bexley on 19 June 1886

BLACKHEATH			BEXLEY		
L. Stokes	b. Clarkson	12	L.A. Shuter	c. and b. J.M. Dale	30
G. Stokes	c. Spottiswoode, b. Clarkson	24	A.M. Oliver	c. Newton, b. Paine	0
F.S. Ireland	c. Friend, b. Jackson	71	W.H. Spottiswoode	b. Druitt	8
G. Dale	b. Oliver	2	J. Shuter	b. Druitt	0
E.B. Ormerod	b. Oliver	0	W.B. Friend	c. Barrow, b. Ireland	10
M.J. Druitt	c. J. Shuter, b. Oliver	14	Revd C.M. Lambrick	run out	1
L. Paine	b. Clarkson	32	G.C. Clarkson	c. and b. Ireland	8
R.S. Barrow	c. L.A. Shuter, b. Oliver	7	E.G. Drew	b. Ireland	0
P.A. Newton	b. Clarkson	5	Cpt. Johnson	b. J.M. Dale	4
J.M. Dale	b. Clarkson	0	Cpt. Pocock	b. Ireland	2
H.G. Hemmerde	not out	0	S.F. Jackson	not out	1
	Extras	14		Extras	3
		181			**67**

Blackheath won by 114 runs.

CLERGY OF ENGLAND (OLD BLUES) V. MCC AND GROUND
Played at Blackheath on 8 July 1886

MCC AND GROUND			THE CLERGY		
Lord George Scott	c. Oldham, b. Sharpe	64	Revd Marsham	b. Druitt	31
E.A. Nepean, Esq.	lbw, b. Greenfield	41	Revd C.M. Sharpe	c. Fothergill, b. Robertson	16
F.S. Ireland, Esq.	not out	109	Revd F.F.J. Greenfield	c. sub, b. Robertson	3
J. Robertson, Esq.	b. Sharp	5	Revd J.W. Marshall	b. Druitt	2
H. Somer-Cocks, Esq.	c. and b. Topham	3	Revd G.T. Oldham	not out	23
Major Fenwick	lbw, b. Topham	0	G.H. Mackern, Esq. (sub)	b. Robertson	0
M.J. Druitt, Esq.	c. Mackern, b. Topham	11	Revd H.G. Topham	b. Robertson	3
G.F. Vernon, Esq.	c. and b. Topham	7	Revd T.N. Rowsell	run out	2
Fothergill	c. Oldham, b. Sharpe	11	A. Hanson, Esq.	b. Druitt	4
Burton	c. Sharpe, b. Topham	12	Revd A.E. Black	b. Robertson	3
F.T. Welman, Esq.	absent	0	G.R. Hutchinson, Esq.	c. Vernon, b. Robertson	3
	b. 19, l.b. 5	24		b. 21, l.b. 1	22
		287			**112**

MCC and Ground won by 175 runs.

185

BLACKHEATH V. SURREY CLUB AND GROUND
Played at The Rectory Field on 7 May 1887

SURREY CLUB AND GROUND			BLACKHEATH		
Abel	b. Druitt	56	H.C. Blaker	b. Abel	9
Smith	c. Lacey, b. Sid Christopherson	5	R.S. Barrow	b. Lockwood	1
Davis	c. and b. Sid Christopherson	3	F.S. Ireland	c. Read, b. Lockwood	0
W.W. Read	b. Ireland	81	J.D. Cruikshank	b. Hulme	1
W.E. Roller	c. Barrow, b. Cruikshank	10	M.J. Druitt	run out	6
Sharpe	b. Stan Christopherson	0	W.F. de Fabeck	lbw, b. Bowley	23
J. Shuter	b. Ireland	16	Stan Christopherson	b. Sharpe	11
Wood	c. and b. Ireland	0	F.H. Lacey	b. Lockwood	0
Bowley	c. K. Christopherson, b. Ireland	8	L. Paine	not out	0
Lockwood	not out	5	K. Christopherson	b. Bowley	0
Hulme	c. and b. Sid Christopherson	5	Sid Christopherson	c. and b. Lockwood	3
	Extras	18		Extras	4
		205			**58**

Surrey Club and Ground won by 147 runs.

Scorer's note: 'M. J. Druitt bowled W.W. Read with a no-ball before he had scored.'

BLACKHEATH V. INCOGNITI
Played at Blackheath, 30 and 31 May 1887

BLACKHEATH	1ST INNS		2ND INNS	
F.H. Lacey	c. Paine, b. Horner	7	c. Martyn, b. Horner	27
Revd G.T. Oldham	c. Paine, b. Horner	5	c. Paine, b. Horner	19
M.J. Druitt	c. Street, b. Horner	24	run out	8
W.F. de Fabeck	b. Paine	14	b. Bonner	4
F.G. Monkland	b. Paine	6	c. Hemming, b. Horner	11
F.S. Ireland	c. Pontifex, b. Horner	26	c. Martyn, b. Horner	9
L. Paine	b. Paine	0	b. Horner	2
K. Christopherson	c. Paine, b. Horner	8	not out	14
R.S. Barrow	run out	1	c. Avory, b. Horner	22
H.C. Blaker	not out	18	c. Hemming, b. Horner	4
C. Kennett	b. Bonner	2	b. Bonner	1
	b. 8, l.b. 3	11	b. 6, w 1	7
		122		**128**

INCOGNITI	1ST INNS		2ND INNS	
G.F. Bonner	c. Monkland, b. Druitt	19	b. Ireland	3
W.E. Martyn	c. Blaker, b. Druitt	3	b. Druitt	23
D.D. Pontifex	b. Paine	0	c. Druitt, b. Ireland	22
H.K. Avory	c. Monkland, b. Druitt	37	st. Lacey, b. Paine	9
C.T. Roller	c. Oldham, b. Paine	0	c. Lacey, b. Paine	12
G.H.P. Street	b. Druitt	12	c. Christopherson, b. Ireland	8
M.H. Paine	b. Paine	32	b. Druitt	9
E.A. Parke	b. Paine	3	b. Druitt	11
C.E. Horner	b. Paine	0	c. and b. Druitt	5
C.J. Ashmore	b. Paine	5	not out	0
A.W.L. Hemming	not out	0	b. Ireland	6
	b. 10, l.b. 3, n.b. 2	15	b. 10, l.b. 3, w 1	14
		126		**122**

Blackheath won by 2 runs.

BLACKHEATH V. O. WYKEHAMISTS
Played at The Rectory Field on 18 June 1887

BLACKHEATH			O. WYKEHAMISTS		
L. Stokes	b. Parr	6	S.J. Wilson	b. Ireland	2
H.C. Blaker	c. Parr, b. Poulton	87	R.S. Barrow	not out	34
E.B. Ormerod	b. Parr	14	C.L. Hemmerde	c. Monkland, b. Cruikshank	9
F.S. Ireland	b. Druitt	41	A.J. Thornton	not out	8
F.G. Monkland	c. Hickley, b. Parr	21	P.C. Parr		
F.H. Lacey	c. and b. Parr	7	C.L. Hickley		
R.D. Budworth	b. Hickley	42	G.W. Burton		
J.D. Cruikshank	c. Parr, b. Druitt	16	D.F. Poulter		
G. Stokes	not out	2	M.J. Druitt		
P. Newton	b. Druitt	0	A.O. Liddell		
F.W. Prior	b. Druitt	4	F.G. Kenyon		
	Extras	46		Extras	7
		286			**61**

Scorecards of a Cricketer

BLACKHEATH V. MCC AND GROUND
Played at Blackheath on 23 July 1887

MCC AND GROUND

A. Worsley, Esq. (sub)	b. Druitt	4
Wheeler	c. Cruickshank, b. Christopherson	18
H.D. Littlewood, Esq.	b. Hemmerde	30
Fothergill	c. Jones, b. Ireland	21
A.C. Macpherson, Esq.	c. Lacey, b. Cruickshank	14
E.T. Gurdon, Esq.	c. Ireland, b. Hemmerde	0
Pougher	b. Druitt	28
H.E.M. Stutfield, Esq.	b. Druitt	9
C.R. Thursby, Esq.	b. Druitt	6
N. Thursby, Esq.	b. Cruickshank	0
P. Laming, Esq.	not out	0
	b. 13, l.b. 4	17
		147

BLACKHEATH

H.C. Blake, Esq.	b. MacPherson	14
F.H. Lacey, Esq.	lbw, b. Pougher	17
F. Stokes, Esq.	lbw, b. Pougher	1
F. Meyrick-Jones, Esq.	st. Wheeler, b. Pougher	11
F.S. Ireland, Esq.	b. Fothergill	5
F.G. Monkland, Esq.	b. Pougher	2
W.H. Pope, Esq.	lbw, b. Fothergill	2
P. Christopherson, Esq.	b. Macpherson	25
M.J. Druitt, Esq.	c. Pougher, b. Fothergill	5
J.D. Cruickshank, Esq.	b. Pougher	2
C.L. Hemmerde, Esq.	not out	2
	b. 2, l.b. 5, n.b. 2	9
		95

MCC and Ground won by 52 runs.

BRYN-Y-NEUADD V. INCOGNITI
Played at Llanfairfechan, 29, 30 and 31 August 1887

BRYN-Y-NEUADD	1ST INNS		2ND INNS	
Brown	c. Smith, b. Druitt	4	c. Rimington, b. Thornton	0
G.F. Wells-Cole	c. Hemming, b. Druitt	9	c. Rimington, b. Druitt	13
H.F. Caldwell	c. Thornton, b. Druitt	38	c. and b. Druitt	21
A.E. Leatham	b. Thornton	39	lbw, b. Cobbold	50
A.T.B. Dunn	c. Pontifex, b. Druitt	3	c. Smith, b. Thornton	14
R.C. Nystrom	c. and b. Thornton	2	run out	13
R. Smith	c. Pontifex, b. Druitt	28	b. Druitt	0
L. Morgan	c. Lake, b. Thornton	4	st. Pontifex, b. Thornton	4
S. Platt	b. Thornton	0	b. Thornton	9
T. Morgan	c. Rimington, b. Druitt	1	not out	12
Eastwood	not out	31	b. Thornton	4
	b. 12, l.b. 6, n.b. 2	20	b. 6, l.b. 4, n.b. 4	14
		179		**154**

INCOGNITI	1ST INNS		2ND INNS	
D.D. Pontifex	b. Brown	0	c. Platt, b. Eastwood	28
W.E. Martyn	b. Brown	37	b. Brown	15
A.E. Gibson	c. Platt, b. Brown	26	c. Eastwood, b. Leatham	0
A.J. Thornton	c. L. Morgan, b. Brown	7	b. Smith	18
M.J. Druitt	st. L. Morgan, b. Leatham	7	c. Leatham, b. Smith	0
E.O. Powell	b. Brown	22	b. Smith	0
Revd P. Hattersley-Smith	c. and b. Brown	13	lbw, b. Smith	14
G.A. Rimington	b. Brown	29	c. Leatham, b. Brown	7
A.W.L. Hemming	lbw, b. Leatham	3	c. Platt, b. Leatham	6
E.W. Lake	st. L. Morgan, b. Leatham	8	b. Leatham	8
C.S.W. Cobbold	not out	23	not out	19
	b. 4, l.b. 2, w 3	9	b. 4, l.b. 5, n.b. 1	10
		184		**120**

Bryn-y-Neuadd won by 29 runs.

BLACKHEATH V. ROYAL ARTILLERY
Played at The Rectory Field on 9 June 1888

BLACKHEATH			ROYAL ARTILLERY		
Lord Harris	c. Curtis, b. Haggard	92	Major Anstruther	c. Ireland, b. Christopherson	36
S. Christopherson	b. King	21	Major Hunter	c. Ireland, b. Christopherson	16
A. Daffen	c. Hunter, b. De Robeck	76	Lieut. Haggard	b. Daffen	0
F.H. Lacey	c. De Robeck, b. Wheble	19	Cpt. Wheble	b. Christopherson	0
R.S. Barrow	not out	30	Cpt. Curtis	run out	54
F.G. Monkland			Cpt. Hall	c. K. Christopherson, b. Christopherson	11
H.C. Blaker	not out	14	Mr C.D. King	c. Ormerod, b. Daffen	6
K. Christopherson			Mr MacMahon	st. Monkland, b. Harris	28
M.J. Druitt			Cpt. De Robeck	b. Daffen	10
E.B. Ormerod			Cpt. Plasit	not out	0
F.S. Ireland			Mr Wray	b. Daffen	0
	Extras	17		Extras	17
		269			**178**

Blackheath won by 91 runs.

BLACKHEATH V. BICKLEY PARK
Played at Bickley Park on 16 June 1888

BLACKHEATH			BICKLEY PARK		
Lord Harris	c. Pattisson, b. Hilder	9	W.H. Patterson	c. and b. Christopherson	5
S. Christopherson	b. Avery	6	J. Marchant	b. Christopherson	28
A. Daffen	b. Avery	10	J.N. Tonge	b. Christopherson	11
F.H. Lacey	c. Fulcher, b. Avery	18	W.B. Pattisson	b. Christopherson	0
R.S. Barrow	b. Hilder	41	W.C. Tonge	b. Christopherson	0
C.L. Hemmerde	c. Hilder, b. Patterson	14	A.W. Fulcher	c. Monkland, b. Christopherson	0
F.S. Ireland	c. Marchant, b. Boosey	51	Revd R.T. Thornton	not out	13
F.G. Monkland	b. Hilder	2	G.C. Boosey	b. Christopherson	0
W.H. Pope	not out	29	C.A.W. Gilbert	b. Daffen	3
C.J. Carver	c. W. Tonge, b. Avery	3	G. Hilder	lbw, b. Daffen	0
M.J. Druitt	lbw, b. Patterson	0	C. Avery	run out	4
	Extras	9		Extras	4
		192			**68**

Blackheath won by 124 runs.

BLACKHEATH V. THE CHRISTOPHERSON BROTHERS
Played at The Rectory Field on 8 September 1888

BLACKHEATH			THE CHRISTOPHERSON BROTHERS		
F.G. Monkland	b. Percy	15	Stanley	b. Druitt	10
G. Woodman	c. Cecil, b. Percy	2	Percy	c. Monkland, b. Ireland	7
R.S. Barrow	c. Stanley, b. Percy	0	Kenneth	c. Monkland, b. Ireland	5
M.J. Druitt	b. Stanley	2	Sidney	c. Woodman, b. Ireland	40
H.C. Blaker	b. Stanley	14	Cecil	b. Druitt	2
J.H.E. Nicolls	run out	2	Malcolm	c. Woodman, b. Ireland	9
R.A. Fegan	c. Sidney, b. Stanley	0	Douglas	c. Monkland, b. R.A. Fegan	8
G.R. Hutchinson	not out	44	Derman (Sr)	b. Druitt	0
F.S. Ireland	c. and b. Sidney	14	Horace	not out	1
J.H. Fegan	c. Percy, b. Stanley	10	Derman (Jr)	b. Ireland	1
	Extras	12		Extras	10
		115			**93**

Blackheath Bowling

	Balls	Mdns	Runs	Wkts
M.J. Druitt	80	4	38	3
F.S. Ireland	79	4	29	5
F.G. Monkland	15	–	9	–
J.G. Fegan	15	1	7	1

Blackheath won by 22 runs.

Bibliography

Aronson, Theo, *Prince Eddy and the Homosexual Underworld* (London, John Murray, 1994)

——, *The King in Love* (London, John Murray, 1988)

Arrowsmith, R.L., *The Butterflies Cricket Club 1862–1962* (Crowthorne, C.T. Hunt, 1962)

Ball, Pamela, *Jack the Ripper: A Psychic Investigation* (London, Arctarus, 1998)

Begg, Paul, *Jack the Ripper: The Definitive History* (London, Pearson, 2003)

——, *Jack the Ripper: The Uncensored Facts* (London, Robson Books, 1988)

Berry, Charles W., *In Search of Wine* (London, Constable, 1935)

Bettesworth, W. A., *Chats on the Cricket Field* (London, Merritt & Hatcher, 1910)

Birley, Derek, *Social History of English Cricket* (London, Aurum, 1999)

Booth, Martin, *The Biography of Arthur Conan Doyle* (London, Hodder & Stoughton, 1997)

Buxton, John, and Williams, Penry, *New College Oxford 1379–1979* (Oxford, New College, 1979)

Cooper, Emmanuel, *The Life and Work of Henry Scott Tuke* (London, GMP, 1987)

Cornwell, Patricia, *Portrait of a Killer* (London, Time Warner, 2003)

Croome, A.C.M., *Fifty Years of Sport* (London, Walter Southwood, 1913)

Cullen, Tom, *The Crimes and Times of Jack the Ripper* (London, Fontana, 1973)

Deacon, Richard, *The Cambridge Apostles* (London, Robert Royce, 1985)

Eddleston, John L., *Jack the Ripper: An Encyclopaedia* (London, Metro Publishing, 2002)

Edwards, Anne, *Matriarch* (London, Hodder & Stoughton, 1984)

Ellmann, Richard, *Oscar Wilde* (London, Penguin, 1988)

Fairclough, Melvyn, *The Ripper and the Royals* (London, Gerald Duckworth, 1991)

Falkus, Gila, *Edward IV* (London, Weidenfeld & Nicolson, 1981)

Farson, Daniel, *Jack the Ripper* (London, Michael Joseph, 1972)

Feldman, Paul, *Jack the Ripper: The Final Chapter* (London, Virgin Books, 1997)

Fido, Martin, *Jack the Ripper* (London, Weidenfeld & Nicolson, 1987)

Field, P.R., and Kimber, I.H., *Felixstowe Ferry Golf Club* (Felixstowe, The Golf Club, 2000)

195

French, Gerald, *The Cornerstone of English Cricket* (London, Hutchinson, 1948)

Frindall, Bill, *England Test Cricketers* (London, Willow Books, 1989)

Frith, David, *By His Own Hand* (London, Stanley Paul, 1991)

Fuller, Jean Overton, *Sickert and the Ripper Crimes* (London, Mandrake, 1990)

Harris, Melvin, *The True Face of Jack the Ripper* (London, O'Mara Books, 1994)

——, *The Ripper File* (London, W.H. Allen, 1989)

Harrison, Paul, *Jack the Ripper: The Mystery Solved* (London, Robert Hale, 1991)

Harrison, Shirley, *The Diary of Jack the Ripper* (London, Smith-Gryphon, 1993)

Higham, Charles, *The Adventures of Conan Doyle* (London, Hamilton, 1976)

Howells, Martin, and Skinner, Keith, *The Ripper Legacy* (London, Sidgwick & Jackson, 1987)

Hyde, H. Montgomery, *Lord Alfred Douglas* (London, Methuen, 1984)

Jobson, Allan, *The Felixstowe Story* (London, Robert Hale, 1968)

King, James, *Virginia Woolf* (London, Hamish Hamilton, 1994)

Knight, Stephen, *Jack the Ripper: The Final Solution* (London, Harrap, 1976)

Lewis, Roy Harley, *Edwardian Murders* (Newton Abbot, David & Charles, 1989)

Lewis, Tony, *Double Century: 200 Years at Lord's* (London, Hodder & Stoughton, 1987)

Lubelow, W.C., *The Cambridge Apostles 1820–1914* (Cambridge, Cambridge University Press, 1998)

Lucas, E.V., *The Hambledon Men* (London, Henry Frowde, 1907)

Malies, Jeremy, *Great Characters of Cricket's Golden Age* (London, Robson Books, 2000)

Martin-Jenkins, Christopher, *Cricket: A Way of Life* (London, Century Publishing, 1984)

Mayo, C.H., *A Genealogical Account of the Mayo and Elton Families* (London, Private, 1882)

Morley, Sheridan, *Oscar Wilde* (London, Weidenfeld & Nicolson, 1976)

Noel, E.B., *Winchester College Cricket* (London, Williams & Norgate, 1926)

O'Donnell, Kevin, *The Jack the Ripper Whitechapel Murders* (St Osyth, Ten Bells Publishing, 1997)

Parris, Matthew, *Great Parliamentary Scandals* (London, Robson Books, 1995)

Paxman, Jeremy, *The English* (London, Michael Joseph, 1998)

Pearsall, Ronald, *The Worm in the Bud* (London, Weidenfeld & Nicolson, 1969)

Perkins, H., *Centenary of Marylebone Cricket Club* (London, MCC, 1887)

Powell-Jones, H.E., *Famous Cricket Clubs* (London, H.F.W. Deane, 1928)

Rait-Kerr, R.S., *A History of Royal Engineer Cricket* (Chatham, Mackays, 1925)

Rennell, Tony, *The Last Days of Glory* (Harmondsworth, Penguin, 2001)

Rice, Tim, *Treasures of Lord's* (London, Collins, 1990)

Ridley, Jane, *The Young Disraeli* (London, Sinclair-Stevenson, 1995)

Rumbelow, Donald, *The Complete Jack the Ripper* (London, W.H. Allen, 1975)

Bibliography

Sainsbury, Maria Tuke, *Henry Scott Tuke* (London, Martin Secker, 1933)

Sharkey, Terence, *Jack the Ripper: 100 Years of Investigation* (London, Ward Lock, 1987)

Sugden, Philip, *The Complete History of Jack the Ripper* (London, Robinson, 1994)

Symons, Julian, *Portrait of an Artist* (London, G. Whizzard, 1979)

Taylor, A.J.P., *English History 1914–1945* (Oxford, Oxford University Press, 1965)

Trow, M.J., *The Many Faces of Jack the Ripper* (Chichester, Summersdale Publishers, 1997)

Tully, James, *Secret Prisoner 1167* (London, Robinson, 1997)

Ward, Andrew, *Cricket's Strangest Matches* (London, Robson Books, 2002)

Wilding, John, *Jack the Ripper Revealed* (London, Constable, 1993)

Williams, Marcus, *The Way to Lord's* (London, Willow Books 1983)

Wilson, Colin, and Odell, Robin, *Jack the Ripper: The Summing Up and Verdict* (London, Bantam Press, 1987)

Wolf, A.P., *Jack the Myth* (London, Robert Hale, 1993)

Index

Index

Index

Index